Look What Other Industry Leaders Have To Say...

"Wow, what an eye-opening book. It's so much better hearing the truth from real players who have been out in the field doing it instead of the regular host of doomsdayers in the media. Thanks for bringing this book to the forefront." – **Matt Furey**, Zen Master of the Internet® www.knockoutmarketing.com

"As my students know, I am big on automating your Real Estate business so your business can work harder than you do. There are many trainers that teach a system, but let me tell you, Mark Evans is a man to emulate. He literally buys and sells property all over the country and is a fulltime world traveler...what a life! You must put "The Insider Secrets of the World's Most Successful Real Estate Investors" at the top of your reading list and learn the success secrets from some of the best minds in Real Estate!" – **Larry Goins**, Author of "The Ultimate Buying & Selling Machine" at www.LarryGoins.com

"Having a Harvard MBA as a partner for the only real estate investor tool which predict the future of housing price values, I've learned one thing. Case studies work. What Mr. Mark Evans has put together is truly phenomenal because he's taken an area (real estate investing) where ordinary people (you know withour Harvard MBAs) have massive success every day and treated the subject in a Harvard MBA way. In fact, I would say, reading 'The Insider Secrets of the World's Most Successful Investors' should come with your own 'Now I Can Make Money' Diploma." **Paulie Sabol**, www.WhenVesting.com

I

D1606320

"This book hits the nail right on the head! It's perfect for any serious Real Estate investor! Whether you're new or experienced, you'll find enormous inspiration and information that you can use to get to the next level! This is sure to be the next great Real Estate best-seller!"
— **Jason Oman**, #1 Best-Selling Author of Conversations with Millionaires at http://FreeMillionaireEbook.com

"What has always impressed me about Mark Evans is his innovative style and constant dedication to improving his business. In this book he has shared secrets from leading real estate investors. What a fantastic opportunity to learn from leaders in the industry. I would highly recommend this book to anyone who wants to create or improve upon a real estate investing business."
-Lou Castillo, www.InvestorRiches.com

Look What Mark Evans DM's Students Have To Say...

"Mark, I truly can't thank you enough! I'm a stay-home mom with three kids who's now on her way to financial freedom. It is so clear to me that this is the work I was always meant to do, and you have made it possible for me to make this leap. I've seen many other books and products out there, but yours is so easy to follow. I didn't have any extra money, and my credit was not that great, yet your personal encouragement and program eliminated the fears that I had about getting started. Anyone can do this if they are motivated to change their lives! Please give your team of wonderful people a huge hug and a 'thank you' for all that you do to guide me through my deals on such a personal basis. I feel very fortunate to be a part of it all. Talk about dreams come true! Thanks again!" **Christine Rupert** in WI

"Mark Evans is a great motivator and educator. Mark makes sense of using all of your resources to create many income streams. His hard-hitting and cutting-edge approach always makes the "light bulb come on" when you listen to him speak. He has personally helped me overcome many challenges in my Real Estate career." **Mynette Boykin** in CA

"The information contained on page 117 alone is worth 1,000 times the price of the book. That one page allowed me to make more money on one deal than I did in 3 months at my full-time job! Thanks for sharing this with us." **Jeremy Blunt** in WI

"I went from playing professional football to having to pawn everything I had and being homeless. Your systems, though, changed it all around for me, and now I'm back in the game and I can see that Real Estate is going to be my path to financial freedom. I can't thank you enough!" **LeRon King** in WV

"Mark Evans stands out as one who has gone through the fire of learning the art of Real Estate Investing, and, now, is so passionately teaching others what he has learned and is cutting our learning curve. His knowledge-packed Real Estate Investing materials are presented in such a concise manner that one has to only read and DO what is taught. It is direct and easy to follow."
Helen Bissette in NC (Retired School Teacher)

"I just wanted to thank you for sharing the ideas in your Reverse Real Estate System. Also, thank you for taking time out of your busy schedule to meet with Nicole and I in Baltimore. From that single meeting, you helped us fix our posture when talking to sellers. Now we only deal with the sellers that NEED to sell not want to sell. We are pre-screening sellers at lightning-speed now. Invariably, that has allowed us to talk to more sellers, which, in turn, allows us to make more offers, which leads to more deals. I look forward to my next meeting where I can view first hand how to automate your system."
Haydn Hislop in MD

THE INSIDER SECRETS

Of The World's Most Successful Real Estate Investors

by MARK EVANS

The Insider Secrets Of The World's Most Successful Real Estate Investors™

© Deal Maker Publishing, LLC

ISBN # 0-9788170-0-1

Printed in the United States of America

This publication is designed to provide competent and reliable information regarding the subject matters covered. However, it is sold with the understanding that the author and publisher are not engaged in rendering legal, financial, or other professional advice. If legal or other expert assistance is required, the services of a professional should be sought. The author and publisher specifically disclaim any liability that is incurred from the use or application of the contents of this book.

Please visit our website at www.MarkEvansDM.com

The author and publisher would like to acknowledge and thank the participants in this book who have granted us permission to cite their trademarked and copyrighted materials and publications.

I first would like to say thank you to my Lord, who has truly blessed me and instilled in me the driving force of excellence.

I am dedicating this book to...

My Grandmother, Reah Evans, who passed on 10/08/05, was such a great mentor to me and a great friend and continues to be a big inspiration in my life, as she is in my heart daily.

To my parents, for their support and encouragement on everything I have done and do. Thank you for that.

To my beautiful fiancé, Deena, for standing by me every step of the way and for the late nights I endured during this project as well for all the other projects that I'm working on.

To my sisters, Brandy and Kimberly for being such beautiful and caring sisters...even though big brother may not say it enough, I love you.

To my beautiful nieces: Payton (6), Samantha (5), Roslyn (3)...every time I see the three of you, I light up, as I'm so excited to see all of you grow and live life to the fullest.

To Vanessa Estadt, who has been my student, friend and left-hand woman and has put many hours into this project, just as she does with all the others...thank you for your commitment.

I love all of you and thank you for all you have given me.

I also want to express my appreciation and dedication to all who have participated in making this book a reality for me. I truly appreciate you sharing your time with me, and I thank you for your commitment to success and for laying a foundation for our readers. Which, then, brings me to you – the reader of this book...

Thank you for supporting me and may you take this book and apply it towards living the life of your dreams. Enjoy every second of life – from the beginning to whatever lies in front of you. May each day bring new opportunities and challenges for you to make it happen and may God bless you.

For most of our readers, I was where you are right now, maybe worse off – broke, no credit and just unhappy. So, this book is for you because it's my turn to give back.

"If you can dream it, you can achieve it." Walt Disney

Table Of Contents

Chapter One

Winner of "The Apprentice"
Kendra Todd is the Season 3 winner of "The Apprentice" as well as the first female winner in the show's history. Kendra's book "Risk & Grow Rich" is a fast and easy read and breaks down risk-taking in Real Estate Investing. Risk is necessary, but there's a way to be smart about it. Here, Kendra talks with me about the challenges she faced early on and how she pushed through them by making smart, educated decisions and weighing the risks versus rewards to get her to where she is today. And where she is today is impressive — she is not only one of the most successful Real Estate Investors and Realtors in Southern Florida, but she is also a celebrated author, lecturer and an award-winning magazine founder. Kendra currently hosts the megahit HGTV series "My House is Worth What?" which helps homeowners across the country get the most equity out of their properties.

Chapter Two

The "Real Estate Rock Czar"
Frank McKinney's two best-selling books **Make it BIG!** *49 Secrets For Building A Life of Extreme Success* and **Frank McKinney's Maverick Approach To Real Estate Success** — *How You Can Go from a $50,000 Fixer-Upper to a $100 Million Mansion* are two must-have books for your Real Estate library. Frank is the creative force behind the world's most opulent mansions built on speculation. Frank is currently in the midst of his latest

and biggest project yet, a $135+ Million dollar oceanfront home. Here, Frank talks with me about the journey he's taken over the last twenty years – from graduating high school with a 1.8 GPA to being a multi-millionaire real estate "artist". He shares what has caused for him to see what's really important and helped him to find his passion for charity, which now includes building homes in Haiti and other third-world countries for the world's most impoverished through his Caring House Project Foundation (www.chpf.org).

Chapter Three

The "New Breed" Investor
Best-selling author of "Buy With No Credit" and "Out Of State Deals" Real Estate Investor and Entrepreneur, TC Bradley, talks with me about how he lost everything in a business deal gone bad. When that happened, TC wasted no time beginning his Real Estate Investing career and developing "New Breed" ways of doing things versus staying with the "old school" mentality. Now, he and Vickie are living the life of their dreams thanks to Real Estate. TC is a true Real Estate Investor who "walks his talk" daily.

Chapter Four

"Million-Dollar-Condo-Guy"
This upstate New York based Real Estate Agent Investor got his start as a kid fixing and selling bicycles to make money. In the mid-1980's, he became a Realtor who was stuck in a rut of working long days, nights and weekends

for a paycheck until, one day, he was suddenly let go from his job. That seemingly unfortunate event ended up catapulting him into the stratosphere of pre-construction condos in Southern Florida, where he now does over $100 Million dollars per year in sales, while working half the amount of time he did as a Realtor who did only $4 Million dollars per year in sales. Here, Doug talks to me about his incredible journey explaining how any Realtor can do the same thing.

Chapter Five

Founder & President, www.WCRT.org
Paul Strauss began his Real Estate Investing career with high hopes...and then his first deal was a bust. Paul talks with me here about what he did next, what choice he made to propel himself forward instead of giving up. Paul explains how that first deal ended up being his most profitable deal because it gave him the motivation to keep going. From there, he was able to become a fulltime Real Estate Investor in just a few short years. Now, Paul is the founder of one of the most successful online networking sites in Chicago.

Chapter Six

"Short Sale Expert"
Gina has been part of the Real Estate world for more than a decade. She got her start in Corporate Relocation, progressed into Real Estate Investing and then earned her Real Estate license. Most recently, she has opened

her own brokerage - Stone Castle Realty. Over the course of the past five years, she has discovered her passion for "Short Sales" after stumbling upon her first one. At that time, she was forced to educate herself only through experience, but she has now taken that experience and created a system — and that system allowed her to simultaneously handle 52 Short Sales, all by herself. Gina talks with me here about how this all came together, how "Short Sales" found her and how she's now able to help so many people with her specialized knowledge.

Chapter Seven

Best-Selling Author of "The E-Myth"

Michael Gerber, the best-selling author of "The E-Myth" series of books , as well as founder and chairman of his world renowned business development company, E-Myth Worldwide, has built an empire by teaching others the value of putting "Systems" in place to run your business so that you don't have to. This vivacious 70-year old didn't even start on his entrepreneurial adventure until he was 41 years old, so no one can ever tell him that they're "too old" to start! In fact, he has coached over 50,000 businesses to success in more than 145 countires! Most recently, he's developed a 2½ day intensive called "In The Dreaming Room" that shows people how to find and nurture their dream until it becomes their reality. This may be the most energy-filled interview I've ever done.

About The Author

Chapter One
Interview with Kendra Todd

Boy, are you in for a treat today. I am getting ready to interview someone that has been such an inspiration to young entrepreneurial people. I'm definitely honored today to be talking to Kendra Todd, who is one of the most successful real estate investors in the country. She is president of www.kendratodd.com and has a commanding knowledge of the real estate industry.

Kendra is a highly acclaimed lecturer, and one of the highest producers of real estate deals in the U.S. She won "The Apprentice" — Donald Trump's reality show on NBC — in Season 3, which made her the first female winner, ever, on that show.

Kendra Todd is also the author of Risk and Grow Rich, where she addresses how to minimize risk and maximize rewards, not only in business but in life as well.

Kendra's mission is to help others reach financial freedom through her tried and true formula. Kendra is dedicated to educating and inspiring others to reach their financial goals and dreams. Now, today, she brings to you her insightful, in-depth knowledge of the real estate world. So, without further adu...welcome, Kendra.

Thank you so much.

How is everything going today, Kendra?

1

Everything is going well. It's just another day of doing deals and helping people get into the real estate investment arena – it's always exciting.

Absolutely. I'm so excited today – I've got my pen and paper and I'm ready to take notes. So, my first couple of questions are about how you became a real estate entrepreneur and about the first deal you did. Can you give us a quick insight into those two things?

Yes, sure. First of all, I totally believe that you have to be looking for some sort of change in your life – you have to be unsettled – to see certain opportunities in front of you.

At the time, when I got into real estate investing, I had started a magazine and publishing company with a few other people. I realized the value of media but also how expensive a start-up company could be. I had a tremendous amount of money going out and very little money coming in.

A problem I think every new business owner faces.

I agree. And everyone I was interviewing for our articles were successful politicians, doctors, attorneys, inventors, etc., but all of their wealth, fundamentally, came through real estate. So, I picked up real estate investing books and began absorbing everything I possibly could. I also went to local investment club meetings.

As I networked, I met someone at one of

2

those clubs who was getting a divorce. He and his wife wanted to unload a property that they had ...a $50,000 condo in Lake Worth, Florida. So, my first deal was a $50,000 property that I purchased "subject to" the existing mortgage, which means that I took over making the mortgage payments for them. But, I did not *assume* the loan – the financing did not go in my name. Essentially, I paid the previous owner a "gifted equity", which basically means that I paid cash for the difference between what was owed on the loan and what my purchase price was.

So, my first deal was a very creative deal. If I had to crunch the numbers right now, I would say that I probably made a 1,000% return on my money on that deal because I put $5,000.00 dollars into it, and, when I sold it, I made about a $150,000.00!

So, on your *first* deal you were a creative real estate investor?

That's correct!

A big key point in there, Kendra, is that, at first, you were interviewing these other people, but then you saw that they found a way to financial freedom through other means rather than what they were trained to do. So, even in the beginning stages, you had to step outside of your comfort zone to get where you wanted to go.

Absolutely. You have to become comfortable with being *un*comfortable, if that makes any sense. A lot of people don't take a step outside into the world and try something new because they feel

3

out of control – I am one of those people. I used to let opportunities pass me by because I wanted to know everything about it before I would go try it. Maybe it was because I was young and inexperienced or maybe it's just that humans don't like change...we don't like to embrace risk.

However, the minute I realized that I was never going to be in control of *all* of the factors of something, and I was able to let go of that, was really when I sort of came alive. I was able to go out there and "exercise my risk muscle", as our good friend Frank McKinney would say, and just go for it. From there, I never looked back. I probably own more properties than I do pairs of shoes – and, for a woman, that's quite a challenging feat.

A buddy of mine always says, "Mark, if you're in your comfort zone, then you're in your failure zone." It's always stepping outside of that zone and getting <u>un</u>comfortable. Now, the more uncomfortable I am, the more comfortable I become – it goes hand and hand.

It's just amazing to me because, once you understand that, the sky is the limit because now you are always taking that step forward. You need to be around people who are do-ers. I mean, look at you, you have been around people who have a *huge* network of people, and all it took was a little bit of energy for you to step outside of your comfort zone. Anyone else can do it too.

That's right. Absolutely.

I think that goes towards the old adage that 80% of becoming successful is just showing up.

4

That's right. You know I believe that it's important to surround yourself with people that have a "can do" attitude because, even if you don't have as much self-confidence as those others, being around those kinds of people is contagious ...it's intoxicating, and it will rub off on you.

Absolutely. It's like when you were growing up...you weren't allowed to hang out with the bad kids because who you hang out with is who you become.

That's right. Robert Kiyosaki says, "If you're not making money with your friends, then get new friends." I know that sounds harsh, but maybe you do keep your old friends – hopefully, you will rub off on *them*. It's very important to surround yourself with people who are constantly re-inventing the wheel and creating new and better ways of doing things.

It's funny you should say that, because what I see a lot of times is that I have opposite friends now than I had 10 years ago. What you find out is that you don't have anything in common with the "old" friends anymore. You can't really talk to them about anything because they just don't "get" it.

I think, for me, one of those proud days was when my mother came to me and she finally saw what an amazing experience real estate investing can be and how you can take command and control over you own financial destiny. She was a believer after seeing that it had worked for

5

me. A lot of people don't want to go out there and put their foot in the water until someone else does it first. My mother has always been skeptical, and she didn't want to take any risks. Now, she's mentoring under someone and is doing deals...it's just incredible.

The thing is that there are a lot of people doing exactly what you just said. They don't even want to get remotely close to the water until someone they know has done it and they can see those results for themselves. A lot of times, though, these people don't see what's going on behind closed doors – working late at night, reading a new book every week, constantly educating themselves, etc. But, of course, that can only go so far too because you have to go out and implement it for it to actually <u>work</u>.

Yes, and you have to constantly learn and go to seminars and network and read books, and do research online. You have to be a sponge because the learning process never ends.

Now, I'm sure you have been exposed to this as well, but I've seen that the more successful you become, the more learning you do.

That's right.

It's almost a catch 22, but it's the truth. It's almost like we're always educating ourselves, but it's because we understand the importance of it. When I first started, I hated reading, but I knew that I had to do it in order to get where I wanted to be.

Another thing that I would like to touch on is networking. It has made me so much money and created some great friends. How about you? Has the power of networking made a difference in your life and business?

What networking has done for me? I have made great friends that way, but, more importantly, I am able to brainstorm with extremely successful people. It is a totally different industry . . . those who are willing to share their knowledge base and vice versa. There are certain principles of business that can be applied to many industries. Usually, you are not going to be able to learn those tricks of the trade – the formulas to success – from your competition. They are not going to sit down with you and help you or give you their "ingredients" to success. But networking forms circles of people that brainstorm together on a regular basis. We share ideas, and that is just incredible.

Yes, networking and applying the ideas immediately from your networking is so key. By surrounding yourself like this, you are surrounding yourself with people who are "can do" people ...these people are out there doing it. It's not as if they are just sitting around talking about it. They are creating ideas. What I have seen, Kendra, through this process, is that money is attracted to speed. If you come up with an idea for a new product, you can make a lot more money because you will take it to your end result much quicker by having your network in place.

That's right. The powerful thing about networking is how you're going to get that first

7

deal. That's how I got my first deal was through networking. There are *lots* of deals that are being done through people networking. There is always that "six degrees of separation", so, as long as you surround yourself with people who you like to work with and who are do-ers – then you can build riches. It is amazing the contacts that you will make and the deals that you will do through networking.

Yes, and I hope people can understand how huge that is – building those bridges. It is just so powerful! Once people understand that concept, they'll just have to get out there and start networking. That is all I did at first. I was networking 5 days a week when I first started. It doesn't necessarily even have to be a real estate related networking event, wouldn't you agree, Kendra? It can be any kind of event because you'll meet a lot of successful people no matter where you go.

Absolutely. A lot of events that I go to are not necessarily real estate related, some of them are just general wealth-building workshops, others are leadership workshops. Others are none of the above. It's amazing how all of the dots will connect – you just have to get out there.

Exactly. If you get anything out of the last couple of minutes, it's that you just have to get out there and *do* it instead of just talking about it. <u>You</u> have to make it happen because no one is going to make it happen for you.

That's for sure. I think we all have a

8

perception of what our limitations are. But, really, we are capable of so much more than we realize. But, you won't know that until you reach your *perceived* limitations and then find the courage and strength to push past them.

Once you are able to do that, you are then able to build a tremendous amount of self-confidence and your "can do" attitude then becomes contagious. From there, you will never look back, and your life will be changed. Picture what you are trying to accomplish – what your goals are, how you define success, etc. – and then go out there and reach that threshold. It's something that will really turn your life in a new direction.

I know. I read your book, "Risk & Grow Rich" several times, actually. I have it dog-eared and underlined because I think that what you touched on is something that a lot of people try to avoid. What I'm talking about is when you say that you have to take risks in order to grow. Can you touch on that a bit more?

Sure. The reason I wrote the book is because I read a lot of books about real estate, and they are all fantastic. I have been inspired. I have learned some tremendous things. But one thing that nobody ever really touches on is the fact that it's scary and intimidating and you *are* going to make mistakes. <u>BUT</u>, it's how you recover from those mistakes that determines who makes it and who doesn't.

You have to have the confidence and the courage to "go there" – fall down, skin a few knees, get back up and continue to keep going.

9

I felt like somebody needed to touch on that because it's something that every new investor can relate to. So, if I can help encourage them to overcome that obstacle of fear and push forward, then I've done something good.

Your book is like walking with them, going through it step-by-step, like you're mentoring them on risk. I know this book will help a lot of people understand risk, and it's got to be very rewarding to know that you've helped people to push through that. In your book, you have really broken down the different kinds of risks. Can you explain that a little more?

Yes. One really, really important thing is that, in order to go out and start to evaluate and command control of your destiny, you have to take risks. But, you need to be able to distinguish between a smart risk and a gamble. There are so many myths about risk, and one is that you have to take a <u>big</u> risk in order to obtain a <u>big</u> reward...but that's not necessarily true.

My book analyzes many different successful entrepreneurs – all of whom are extraordinary through the combination of taking many small risks that all added up and turned into one really huge reward! You just have to know the difference between taking a gamble and taking a smart risk, because there is certainly a big difference.

There is a very big difference, and you do an excellent job of explaining it in full detail in your book.
So, How about now we talk about the biggest mistakes people entering into business

make. Where do you think they drop the ball? Where do you think they are continually messing up as they go through the growing process?

I've seen that one of the things people stop doing is educating themselves. Part of being a smart risk-taker is knowing how to evaluate and weigh the odds versus the potential rewards... being able to see if the risk is worth taking. In order to do that, you have to be educated, you have to be informed and you have to be in-tune with your industry for whatever risk you are trying to take. By not continuing to learn, you lose that momentum and get caught up in whatever it is that you're doing, and you've got to keep an eye on those risk factors.

I have interviewed a lot of very successful entrepreneurs, and the common theme that I have pulled from every single one of those interviews was the fact that, looking back, they all said they wished they would have trusted their gut instincts more. I don't think people, in general, trust their gut instincts nearly enough. In the beginning, though, when you're just stepping out, you're probably not going to have as many gut instincts when it comes to figuring out the "smart" risk from the foolish one.

But, as you go out and take those first baby-steps, you'll then start to walk, then you run and then you start jumping! You are going to develop intuition – you have to trust that intuition. Some people second-guess it, and that's what leads to missed opportunities and potential failures. You really need to see failure as an obstacle to get above, under, through or around as fast as possible. As long as you don't see failure as an

11

end result, you'll always have the courage to get back up and keep going.

The key here is, we all fail daily. However, failing does not mean you are a failure. Michael Gerber says he wakes up and fails as quickly as possible so that the rest of his day will be a breeze. We are all going to have obstacles as business people and as growing entrepreneurs. It's like you said, though, how you react and recover from that situation is what makes the difference. You can't just lay there and cry about being a failure... get up, brush yourself off and call the people that you surround yourself with to get a little bit of encouragement because sometimes that does help.

Then, look at it totally different — most times, it's not even that big of a deal. It's probably not what you were wanting to achieve anyway. Then, you can look back on it and learn from it.

Right...don't sweat the small stuff. Mark, most people think *everything* is a big deal. That's the difference between a successful entrepreneur mindset and some people that may not reach that higher level of success in business. You need to have the ability to recognize that mistakes have *value*. As long as you <u>learn</u> from them, you'll be ok. I think we lost that childlike mentality of "riding a bike".

I know it sounds very simplistic, but it's true. When you're a small child, and you get on your bike with training wheels, you know that one day Mom and Dad are going to take the training wheels off. You want to learn how to ride that bike so bad that it's worth taking the risk of falling...

and, nine times out of ten, you will fall at least once or twice. But, you'll give it a shot anyway because the results are worth it.

If we could apply that same passion, that same desire, for "riding the bike" to how we approach our businesses, then we would all be very successful.

There is no better feeling than taking the training wheels off and becoming free, and, when you take control of your life, you create your own destiny, and you get to leave that legacy, which is such a free feeling. What I did when I started out was I wanted to become as successful as I could for the others in my family, like my nieces and my parents, so that I could surround them with a "financial freedom wall". As I did that, I took myself out of the equation because I was too emotionally attached. I started working so much harder when I did that because I saw things differently, does that make sense?

Absolutely.

I think that by doing that and having that mindset, it minimizes how you see risk differently than others.

We take risks every day — and we don't perceive them as necessarily being right — but other people are scared to death. It's like some people are scared to death to fly, even though the odds of dying in an airplane are much less then dying in a car accident. Yet, we know that we have to get from point "A" to point "B", and our car is our vehicle to get us there, so we don't

13

even think about it, we just take that risk.

For an entrepreneur it is the same way... there are certain risks that are musts. There is no choice. You have to be able to get from point "A" to point "B". Successful entrepreneurs are always going to take that vehicle to get there because it has to be done in order to reach the goal.

It's interesting...when I interviewed people for the book and talked about how some people perceive risk, it's amazing what you will do when you know you have to do something in order to get somewhere in life or in business. The perception of risk, at that point, is minimized, and you just do it.

Exactly. Another thing I see, Kendra, is that a lot of people wait too long. They go to seminars, they get excited and then they try to get from point "A" to point "Z" overnight — kind of like an overnight success. Unfortunately, it just isn't feasible to think that way.

No, it's not.

Success is a process. It's like you said, you are constantly building your risk muscle. You surround yourself with different people as you grow. As you start implementing all these pieces, things just start happening from "A" to "B", and then you might get to "D" without going to "C" first or whatever...it's a process.

That's why I was so excited about getting to talk to you because it's hard to find people who really like to talk about what we have to do to be entrepreneurs. Can you talk about some of the challenges of being a young person — either young

To Receive Your $247 In Free Bonuses: www.TheInsiderSecretsGifts.com

in age or young at heart – and getting into the real estate business? What kinds of challenges has Kendra Todd faced? Just touch on a couple of the challenges that you see daily...

I guess, looking back, it was when I was 23 (and looked like I was about 18!), I was afraid of, "Who is going to listen to an 18-year old talk about building financial freedom?" I ran into a lot of challenges back then because, in order to be successful, you have to establish a certain level of trust with anybody that you do business with...and certainly when you are trying to negotiate a real estate deal. You have to have that "trust factor" – it's essential – or else you're not going to be able to negotiate any terms that are going to make the deal worthwhile. And you being young...or just being perceived as young – it's unfortunate, but, in our society, people don't think that there are young people out there that know what they're doing or how to manage finances or deals, etc., and so a lot of people aren't willing to take a risk with trusting a young person.

I certainly did run into that challenge too, but the minute people realized that I had self-confidence and that I knew what I was talking about, all of that diminished. This is because people with self-confidence are contagious. It doesn't matter how old or how young you are, people like being surrounded by other people like that. There are lots of ways to overcome that challenge.

Also, a lack of experience is a challenge. You know you're going to make a lot more mistakes in the beginning than you will as you go along. There will usually be more mistakes and smaller

15

mistakes – hopefully you don't know enough to be dangerous! The point is that most people quit before they begin – they give up too soon.

I see that so much. There are all these infomercials that promise millions of dollars in 30 days, but if that was really true, everyone would do it. So, when they don't get the million dollar paycheck – or even $1,000 paycheck – as soon as they think they should, they give up. Really, that's the time to push harder and further ahead.

It's not hard making money by investing in real estate, but you do have to get to a certain point where you've built up your momentum in order to really be on a roll. You have to put in the time, you have to have the dedication and you have to be willing to make a lot of mistakes in the beginning. Hopefully, you reach a certain point where you will have it on auto-pilot, but its going to take patience and dedication to get there, so don't give up before you begin.

Yes. That is so key – patience and dedication. I always relate it to a football game. A lot of these guys and gals are at the one-yard line, ready to score and when they fumble they can regain control and score, but most just leave the ball park and quit. The point here is that you're going to fumble the ball, but how you react to the fumble to get that touchdown is determined by you. What I have seen from past experience is that when I get the most resistance is when the best things happen. When I get that resistance, I contact people who have gone through that resistance – aka my mentor or mentors at the

16

time. I contact them, and they talk to me and guide me through it by reassuring me that it's going to be ok...they hold my hand and walk me through the process.

Another thing that you touched on that I think is important is mentors. I have associates that make $2 million a year, and are in their mid-fifties and they still have mentors that they call before they do any deals. Their mentors might be younger than them, their own age or even older, but you should always have a mentor.

You should always have someone that you can call upon to analyze a deal, even if you're at the level of success you want to be or are making millions of dollars – whatever your goals are. There are reasons why those people are ultra-successful ...it's because they follow certain principles. Remember, you're never too old to have a mentor. You're never going to know *everything*. Always remember that there will always be somebody out there that knows a little bit more, so let them guide you.

Absolutely. Having a mentor isn't just for real estate – it could be for marketing or for self-improvement or for negotiating...it could be for a bunch of different things. So, when you're picking out your mentor, just keep all of your options open. Don't shut anybody out until they sit and explain what they can help you with. I can tell you that, if I didn't have mentors, I would not be here with you today.

Kendra, you said something about all the people you interviewed...it didn't matter if they were making $2 million a year, they still

have mentors. Of course they do because they understand the importance of it – it is so key. I see so many people skimping around thinking that they are saving money by not investing in a mentor or in a program that can guide them through the steps. That **IS** where you need to invest your money, but also keep in mind that not all mentor programs are created equal.

Make a smart decision, gather information and see what's going on around them. See what kind of success their students are having, and then start getting involved with what they are doing. I call it "becoming a person of value".

Mark, becoming a person of value is so crucial to succeeding in business.

I know that when I first started, I didn't have a lot of money, so what I would do was buy the cheapest product from the mentor that I wanted to have – just to show him that I respected him and what he was doing. I knew this would start the relationship-building process to show him that I was serious, and then...boom...next thing you know, you're on the phone with him a year later or maybe even 3 months later, whatever it may be. But, becoming that person of value and working with mentors is such a huge key to success. I have several mentors now.

I also wanted to talk about the fact that so many people get into real estate investing with their whole goal being that they can, one day, quit their job and get rid of that paycheck. Can you touch on that? I know you talk about this in your book – that people are afraid to give up the steady paycheck. They want the security of that

18

steady paycheck that you get in a J-O-B.

One of the things I press into people is *not* to quit your job and go out and invest in real estate because you have to have money coming in. I see that happen all of the time, and I'm sure you see it all of the time to Mark. You hear, "I quit my job, and now I'm going to be an investor".

I always ask the question, "Well, when you quit your job, were your investments paying you more each month than your job was?" Then, they just look at me blankly. You can't make that mistake, and I see it all of the time.

What is important is what you do with the money that you <u>do</u> make. You don't *have* to quit your day job – some people never do. Some people's goals are to get out of the nine to five grind or, in my case, the nine to twelve grind. What is important is what you do with the money that you earn. Eventually, if your goal is to quit your nine to five job – then you will be able to do so without wondering how the bills will get paid.

The one thing that I <u>will</u> stress, without going into to much detail – I'll leave some of the mystery to the book – but it is to make sure that, before you make the move to quit your job, be sure that your investments are stable and solid... be sure that you can cover your monthly income over the long-term.

I call it "creating a monthly residual". Like you said, "stabilizing your monthly income". The book is awesome, Kendra. You covered this so thoroughly in your book. Where can our readers go and get your book "Risk & Grow Rich" that we've been talking about?

My website is www.kendratodd.com. They can also buy the book at www.kendratodd.net or go to www.amazon.com – wherever you can buy books is where you can find my book.

It's a great, easy read, so get over there and get her book.

Kendra, what are some other points that you can shine the light on to help get people from point "A" to point "B"? I know we have talked about taking risks, getting mentors and networking – what else?

Let's talk about the biggest key to your success on your first deal – I would like to go back to that. Were you scared when you did your first deal?

Not really – I wasn't scared at all. I thought I would be, but the reason I wasn't was because I had surrounded myself with people who were doing deals, so I knew it would work...I just had faith. I had the blessing and opportunity, beforehand, to be around people that were mentoring me and giving me encouragement. Most people don't have that, and I think that is where some of the fear comes in. Not everyone has people in their lives saying, "This is a great deal for you." They were encouraging me about what a great deal it was, so I got excited about it.

But, I will tell you that it took me an awful long time to get to that point – a lot longer than most people. I had a lot of fear for a lot longer than I wish I had. I let a lot of deals pass me by. So, by the time I got through that first deal...well, there was nothing else to be scared about.

20

That is one of the most important parts of the book...don't let opportunity pass you by. If only I would have gone out there and said, "You know what...I have enough faith in myself and know that this is great deal," If I'd have done that, I would have had a few more really great deals under my belt earlier. But, somebody else got those deals. So, by the time I got to my first deal, it was really overdue.

Your first deal you did...you were 23 years old, you said?

Yes, I was 23.

That's awesome. Since we're on the age thing, can you talk a little bit about being a young entrepreneur...about how, when you're out there doing it, people will listen. They might look at you a little differently, at first, but if you say you'll do something and you actually do it, things will start happening...it is almost impossible for things to *not* start happening. By being young, I actually think we have an advantage because the entrepreneur will see themselves in you. Does that make since?

Yes. It's important to pass on all of the knowledge that you have gained to someone who can, hopefully, absorb it and implement and maybe make a few less mistakes than you did because of what you have shared with them. It's like you said, Mark, build a legacy. Successful people want to pass on what they have learned. They don't want their legacy to just end with them, and that's half the reason why entrepreneurs are

21

so driven. For some, it's just the money but for many it isn't...money is just the aftermath. I think it's the legacy you want to leave behind that's important. There are so many people out there willing to take people under their wings because it just creates a better world.

Not only that, but it's like you said when you were interviewing all of those people...you never hear anyone say, "I wish I would have waited until later to start." When you're young, that's when they want to reveal this information to you, as a mentor. They can't wait to instill this information in you because you're fresh and can take it in easier. It's really tough to get that light shined on you and to get someone to help you out because, in the beginning, you don't know who to contact.

As an entrepreneur, it's so much easier and clearer. We have so many things going through our heads...we call it "the idea factory". Getting people in place to do this and do that...and getting the light shined on it just makes it so much easier.

Kendra, I know you wanted to talk about some opportunities that you have going. What is it that Kendra Todd is doing these days, after you have done these real estate deals? You have had great success with the book and your many projects, so what are you working on now? What kind of projects can you talk about?

One of the things I do in my business is I try to be the researcher and try to locate all of the investors out there that are looking for the next "hot spot" or the next "up swing" area. A

22

savvy investor is willing to do a deal anywhere... they know they could even find a deal in San Francisco.

But, for most people, it falls back onto being in the right location — and with location I'm not talking about waterfront or golf course. I'm talking about being in the right city, in the right town, and the right place at the right time. If you are in the right place at the right time, it can increase your return on your money exponentially.

I do lots of market research on my deals. I study job-growth statistics. I study trends in the housing market. I study affordability — what you can get for your money. I study all of these things, as I'm always looking for the next hot spot.

How cool. It is about location, but it's also about so much more, and people don't always see that part of it.

Part of my investing formula, too, is that I keep my price-points under $300,000. I have only invested in one property where I broke my rule, and there were extenuating circumstances. Every other deal that I have done, I have kept all of my deal prices low because I like lowering my risk by lowering my carrying costs, etc. and there is more chance for appreciation and more chance for success this way. This strategy just works really well for me.

Luckily, some of the deals that didn't match up to my formula and that I didn't do, I am really glad now that I didn't do and that I walked away. But, we are moving into a new market. We have some really great opportunities in North Carolina... in the mountain region of North Carolina and also

23

on the coast. The reason is that they are not building anymore waterfronts, and there are still areas in the eastern part of the United States where you can get an affordable waterfront property. I think that's important because areas are going to appreciate and catch up to their more expensive neighbors to the North and South.

I have also been doing a lot of studying in the Santa Fe, New Mexico market, and I have my eye on Boise, Idaho. I'm looking into Tennessee. I'm looking into the markets where baby boomers and retirees are moving to.

If you don't mind, you talked about walking away from an opportunity earlier. How important it is to understand that there is always another deal around the corner? Some of the best deals you can do are the ones you _never_ do.

That's right. You learn so much just by doing the studying beforehand. I think we all learn a lot more in life by eliminating ones off the list than we do by doing things right the first time.

Yes, and that is so important. These are all the important pieces of the puzzle. That is why we are committed to doing these interviews with successful people who are do-ers, not just talkers.

Another thing, Kendra, is systems. What have systems done for your business? I know your schedule is just outrageous, so can you talk about what systems work for you and how important they are to your success?

It's funny that you bring that up because I really struggled for a long time because of not having or implementing a system. And then I got one. You know you're successful when you leave, and your company is still running and making as much money as it was when you were there. If you don't have those systems in place, then you *are* the company, and you're not really a business-owner – you're really just self-employed.

It has always been so crucial to me to build the right systems and put them in the right place because then you know that you have all of these moving parts, and, if one person leaves, then all you have to do is plug one person back into that place and the system continues to run – that way you rely more on the system than you do on the people who are working the system.

Even though systems are very important, it is also crucial to have the right team. You have to have the right people, but, if you don't have the right system in place, then it is almost like being a really bad basketball coach with the best players in the country. You won't win a game unless you have the right leader and the right system and the right strategy and the right players.

Kendra, are you familiar with Michael Gerber, the author of "The E-Myth"?

I have read that book.

That is what he talks a lot about is not working yourself into another job, but working yourself into owning a company.

That's right. Don't be the person that bakes

25

the pies until 2am, goes to bed, and then gets up and does it all over again.

Exactly. Once you understand that, then you know your goal. Our goal is to make a bunch of money, retire (ok, I'm never retiring!) and do what we want. To allow yourself to do the things that you want, you need to be able to hand it off to a person that you can trust...that's the ideal. But, until you have your systems in place, you have no idea what kind of employee you are looking for.

You have to make sure that you don't have the, "If I want something done right, then I have to do it myself" attitude, because then you will never grow.

Yes, and keep in mind that no one will *ever* do it as good as you. But that doesn't matter because the system will do it for you. Just implement the system and work the process. Honestly, I think my job is just to be a straight marketing person. I love marketing, and that is what we do . . . we market the system, and the system works to go out and get the deals. Then, you can spend your time doing what you want to do, right, Kendra?

That's right.

Spend your time doing what you are best at, because we're not all good at everything. I want everyone to understand something...I know that what I have done in the past is to sit down and write out what my weaknesses are and what my strengths are. Then, I'll sit myself down in front of the people who can help me with my weaknesses.

I have the tendency to do everything myself, but that leaves me spreading myself too thin around the company. My ideas thrive when I can dedicate time to new business ventures and opportunities. I have since surrounded myself with people who compliment my work ethic and attitude. It's so important to have a competent team around you. Now, don't get me wrong, knowing each department of your business and how it runs is very important, but you don't want to be completely dependent on anyone when it comes to your own survival. When things break down, I have to know how to fix the problem myself. My team allows me to generate new thoughts and new ideas that lead to successful systems and opportunities.

You guys have teamed up in South Florida, and are making some very neat things happen.

I would like to talk next about how our readers can get a hold of you to take the next step and to see the opportunities that you are always presenting. What would be the process for our readers to do to get a hold of you and take the next step?

They can visit us on the web at www.kendratodd.com or they can always give our office a call at 561-819-5784. There is always somebody there to take your call.

There is one thing that I take pride in, and it's having awesome opportunities available that really reduce your risk because I am not a "flipper", I am a long-term real estate investor. I always have unique properties and opportunities, like I have mentioned.

It is becoming more and more difficult to create a monthly cashflow and buy property that has the appreciation as well as cashflow. The real estate market has just gone crazy these last few years, and we have had to change and adjust our strategies for investing because of it. So, now I can provide people with opportunities where they are going to eliminate risk for a year, two years, or even three years...I love doing deals like that! We have deals like that available just about all over the place! Your readers can contact us to find out more about all of our deals through our website...again, at: www.kendratodd.com.

So, make sure you get over to www.kendratodd.com and subscribe to her newsletter so you can keep up to date with her awesome opportunities. Kendra, I'd like to ask you what you think is the single most important quality of someone who wants to embrace success?

Passion. If you're not passionate, then you're not going to have that fire in your belly to go out there and find something. You have to be on a mission, and you have to know why you are making this change in your life. If you don't have passion, then you will eventually give up. If you don't have passion, then you really don't want that "something". Passion brings success.

Absolutely. What are your thoughts on people saying "I want to retire." To me, there is no passion in retiring at all. Do you agree?

Yes, I do. There IS no passion in retiring. You will never retire, but it's not because you can't, it's because you love what you do and you love making your life what it is.

I could never figure that out...who really wants to retire and golf or do nothing every single day? It might be fun for a week or even a month, but then it's going to get old. And if you know you're living to your fullest potential because you are so passionate about it, why retire?

There is nothing that can stop you. You are always learning and spreading your legacy on to others. Kendra and I...our goal is to continuously be leaving a legacy by helping others grow, including everyone that is reading this book now. You can do this too. The great thing about what Kendra and I do is that we do it because we <u>want</u> to, and I think that is huge!

Frank McKinney always talks about how important it is to instill your knowledge into others as you learn. Educate and learn more yourself and then get it in front of others to give them guidance.

Kendra, do you have any other words or thoughts that you would like to talk about before we wrap this up?

Just go out there and get involved – I just can't say it enough. If you're reading this, maybe you're one of those people who just hasn't "gotten in the game" yet. Well, you know what...just go for it! You *are* going to make some mistakes, but if you don't go out there and give it a shot, then you will never know. You don't want to be one

29

and says, "Man, I really wish I would have gotten into this game a lot sooner. I thought about it for years, but I keep letting the opportunity pass me by."

I guarantee you that when you do your first deal and you see yourself start to get on that path to financial freedom, you will feel sick to your stomach that you didn't get into it sooner. So, don't fill your life full of regrets, just go out there and do it...take risks, but make them educated risks.

Absolutely. Once again, you have got to get Kendra's book called "Risk and Grow Rich". You can also get a hold of Kendra at: www.kendratodd.com.

I appreciate you taking the time to speak with me, Kendra, and I hope you have a great day.

Thank you for having me.

You're welcome. Until next time.

Chapter Two
Interview with Frank McKinney

Hello, everyone. I'm really excited about the interview we're about to do. This is a person that I've looked up to and been inspired by for a long time. Without his unique approach about continuously flexing my "risk muscle" to move forward, I would not be doing this interview. So, with that being said, make sure you listen clearly and take down a lot of notes on the points that he makes because they are very powerful, and you'll want to grab onto every word so that you can begin your "Maverick" journey today! Ok, let's get this started...

Frank, I know you've got a busy day, so I just want to give you a quick introduction and get this going. How does that sound?

I'm ready when you are.

Today, I'm so excited to have Frank McKinney — a guy I've hung out with, looked up to and who inspires me daily. Not just to make money, but to help other people get to the next level.

So, who is Frank McKinney? Frank McKinney is a two-time, international best-selling author and visionary who sees opportunities and creates real estate markets where none existed before. His two best selling books are Make it BIG! *49 Secrets For Building A Life of Extreme Success* and Frank McKinney's Maverick Approach To Real

Estate Success – *How You Can Go from a $50,000 Fixer-Upper to a $100 Million Mansion.*

His 20-year career began with a $50,000 fixer-upper home, and his latest project is the largest and most expensive "spec" home ever created at $135+/- million dollars. Mr. McKinney was recently featured on ABC's 20/20, the cover of USA Today, the Oprah Winfrey Show, CBS and The Early Show, just to name a few.

Mr. McKinney has a unique look, a disarming personality and a willingness to attempt what others won't even dream of, which has earned him the nickname of the "DareDevil Developer" and the "Real Estate Rock Czar" – all by using his Maverick Approach to real estate investing.

Mr. McKinney now spends a tremendous amount of his time on philanthropic causes, specifically, his Caring House Project Foundation. In 1998, Frank and Nilsa McKinney founded The Caring House Project Foundation, a non-profit, 501C3 organization that provides housing for homeless families in South America, the Caribbean, Indonesia and here in the U.S. For this reason, he has become one of the most successful real estate investors in the world, as well as one of the largest humanitarian forces out there.

I respect his work, both in real estate and in his charity a great deal, and I know that you will gain huge benefits by hearing his story. So, I'm both honored and privileged to have Frank McKinney with me today. Mr. McKinney, welcome!

Mark I want to first start off by acknowledging you and thanking you for your commitment to our Caring House Project

32

Foundation. I was reading an article today about how Bill Gates is stepping away from Microsoft to spend more time with charity after 33 years of Microsoft. Although he still seems pretty young, I think that, at a certain point in our life, we should all look to do something so great as to build up a great company – build up a nice big fortune – and be able to share it with those less fortunate, and that's becoming a big part of my life. You certainly have supported our Caring House Project Foundation efforts in Haiti and in Nicaragua and Honduras. So, for that, I thank you, and I want to give you all I've got for the next hour.

Excellent. Thank you, Frank. I wanted to start right off with what the common theme of this book and interview is going to be. I know you've spoken a lot about how to focus just on one deal and how important the first deal really is, just to get started. Can you shine the light, here, and give people your background story...who Frank McKinney is, and where he started.

Sure. Let's just start with a little, brief bio...maybe why readers should spend the next 20 minutes reading this and focusing in on what I have to say because I started my real estate career 20 years ago...May 19, 1986.

As you mentioned, Mark, it all started with that first fixer-upper – that first $50,000 crack house. It was a drug dealer's house in a really bad part of town in West Palm Beach, Florida. We had this notion that, no matter where we were working, we were going to make that crack house...the first house – the nicest, little house on the block.

33

Now, I didn't have the benefit of pursuing a formal education, based upon my lack of application in high school. So, I left high school with a 1.8 grade point average and moved way down to Florida when I was 18. I had a job digging sand traps by hand on a golf course, and then I was a maintenance guy on a golf course and then a maintenance guy on tennis courts and then I even became a tennis pro for a while – I was a teaching tennis pro.

So, you never even had any idea about real estate investing...what it was or how to do it?

No, I sure didn't. I guess my first epiphany moment when I moved from "the nine to five" into real estate investing full-time was when I was a tennis pro. I was teaching very affluent people how to hit a fuzzy, yellow ball across the net better. It dawned on me that these people had the leisure time to pay me $50 per hour to learn how to play tennis better – to really spend most of their day doing things that they enjoyed. That was very impressionable to me, as a young 20-21 year old. They were driving up in fancy cars...getting out of the car with the best tennis clothes on, and kissing a beautiful wife goodbye...that whole American dream that we see represented and, especially as young people, we want to attain.

A lot of people do want that lifestyle, but they don't know how to get there or how to apply themselves to move forward towards it.

True. I learned that their fortunes weren't... well, they may have started in "the nine to five" like most people. You know, nobody's born a real estate investor. You don't go to school to become a real estate investor. You get with people like Mark Evans and make them your mentor and have them teach you how to become a real estate investor.

People like Mark weren't around when I was younger, and I had to learn from my mentor, who was actually my student at the same time. The people I was teaching tennis to taught me about real estate, and that's how they made their fortunes. So, I believed that Florida, being a very transient community...there's still 1,000 people moving into Florida every week...that I could make a living here buying distressed properties.

So, in essence, having mentors in your life is so important that it will cut so much time off you trying to learn it all yourself.

Frank, did you ever dream that you'd be doing million dollar homes?

I will tell you that I had no dreams of doing million dollar homes when I got started. And I think that's the first lesson...dreams are wonderful, but that's all they are until you make them come true, and so I was a do-er, not a dreamer. The do-er in me started with that first $50,000 house, and that's all I cared about.

Mark's really good at what he does as far as mentoring, but there are a whole lot of ways of making real estate investing a reality and a whole lot of other ways to teach people how to make real estate investing a reality. But, he can't possibly teach them all, and it would be hard for him to say which way is best for any one person.

35

What I find kind of disheartening with today's real estate investor is they don't give their initial application any thought. What I mean by application is: are you going to be a wholesaler, are you going to be a retailer, are you going to be a short-seller, are you going to be a builder, are you going to be a rehabber? You need to pick one and stick with it.

The best way I know how to do that is to start with that one...that first piece of property. Don't be thinking about the second one because, I can guarantee you, if you lose money or you don't make enough money to match the effort that you put in, then you're not going to like the real estate business. Then, you may try jumping into wholesaling and then retailing and then flipping... and then 5-10 years down the road, you look at yourself and say, "What have I accomplished?" The answer will be nothing.

Frank, that is such a key point and why so many people give up or say "it doesn't work"... but it's really only because they weren't focused enough.

In my first book, I talk about taking the "lunch pail approach". That's just a real simple concept for me to grasp, as an uneducated guy who graduated high school with a 1.8 grade point average. Just pack a lunch pail — figuratively or literally, it's up to you. But, pack it and show up everyday, day in and day out, working on your first project, making it a success.

And, now, 20 years later...yes, we're building a "spec" home that's going to be the worlds first nine-figure, $125+/- million for a

36

"spec" house. I never set out to do that. I just set out to make that first $50,000 one the nicest one on the block.

There were a lot of big, key points in there, Frank...the first deal. However, I see so many people that start on their first deal, but, at the same time, they're already focusing on the next one before they even finish the first. When that happens, they lose focus and, like you said, they can't match up their efforts with how much they make. Then, a lot of times, they decide that real estate investing is "just not for them" anymore.

The danger, Mark, is that the younger generation – and even some people who have been around for a little while – are tempted by that adage of "get rich quick" that they see on infomercials. The sooner you get it in your mind that real estate is not one of those businesses, the better you will do. It just doesn't happen. Now, you might get lucky once and wholesale a property and make some quick money. But, if you don't take a long-term approach to your real estate investing, well...like in the stock market, you need to take a long-term approach, in commodities investing, you need to take a long-term approach, and, even with your own your house, you need to take a long-term approach.

Real estate investing is no different. The waters have been muddied a bit with a lot of these "guru" guys going out and talking about how you can make money overnight with no money down, etc. There are ways to make profits with no money down. I don't knock that, I'm just not an advocate of debt because, to me, that's just

37

another four-letter-word. But, there are certainly ways to get into real estate investing without any money down, but you will still need to take that long-term approach and just focus on the one, single property you're working on at that time.

It's so hard, though, for people who are desperate for cash now to not get caught up in all that hype. What I have seen is that those are the same people who will end up quitting the real estate business and saying it doesn't work, a lot of times.

You will be tempted as a human being to want to jump from one application to the next. If you do that, though, that's no way to build a legacy – and I'm talking about in terms of your net worth, what you can do for humanity, what you can do for those who are less fortunate than you...it just ain't going to work!

It took me some years to understand that. My first years in business, I was just focused on the bottom-line. But, at the same time, it was by accident that I was only focused on the bottom-line. I was doing only one or two projects at a time until I was ready to grow beyond that.

And that could bring us to the next point, Frank. I know you talk about this a lot...exercising your "risk muscle". Once you do get past that scary part and the first deal...you get all those jitters out. What does it take to go from a $50,000 house to over a nine-figure house in twenty years?

Mark, the business you're really in...I mean, yes, you're really successful in real estate

38

but, for the purpose of this interview and what you do with your students…it's the "fear removal" business. You could be selling tires to people — it doesn't matter — it's the fear that has to be mitigated. It's never going to go away. I have to admit that I'm afraid everyday when I wake up. Some days I'm very anxious when I wake up. That feeling in the pit of your stomach like, "Oh my gosh, is this $125 million house ever going to sell? Oh my goodness, is this $50,000 house ever going to sell?" Fear is a wonderful motivator, but it can also be, and more often it is, a horrible inhibitor.

You're right…it holds so many, too many, great people back from reaching their dreams.

What I talk about in both books — my favorite chapter and absolutely the most well-received chapter in both books — is that, just like exercising your risk muscle to make it stronger and be able to withstand greater pressure in business, you have to apply this to your life, in general, too.

Without that approach to life, Mark…it doesn't matter if somebody's reading this today who has no desire to get into real estate, but who wants to, instead, host a Tupperwear party at their house once a month. We all have to embrace fear. The primary difference between my real estate career and most others' is my ability to deal with the fear and anxiety and get past the "should I step out from behind my nine-to-five desk and take a chance".

There are people reading this and people that I've met that are a lot more "on the ball"

39

when it comes to education and pure intellect, and. So, when it comes to real estate, they should be succeeding at a higher level then me. But, most of them that I've seen – looking them square in the eye – they're held back by their fear.

We all have fears, Frank. I still have fears I have to overcome all the time. One of my biggest fears is public speaking, but I faced it and am getting more comfortable with it all the time. I know that I will propel myself farther ahead if I get over that fear.

There's a great book I'd like to recommend about fear. If you go to my website at www.Frank-McKinney.com, and you go to Frank's Top Ten Reading List...there's actually 15 or 16 books on there by now. A great book there is written by a philosopher by the name of Anthony De Mello. He touched on fear in this way, and I thought it was just so great.

We've been taught our entire lives that we fear the unknown. We fear what we don't understand, and getting into real estate or doing that first deal or getting beyond that first deal and maybe going to a higher price point or doing more than one deal, then two, then three, the fear of quitting the nine-to-five...we're stopped by that fear.

What De Mello says is, "How can you fear something that you don't know?" Think about that. How can you fear something that you don't know? It's not possible to fear something that you don't know. What we fear is not the unknown but the thought of leaving the known, what we *do* know.

That's a powerful statement...people need to go back and read that again.

We fear leaving the nine-to-five. We fear from getting out from behind our desk. We fear taking that first chance...because we don't want to leave what we're comfortable with. That is the most important message, regardless of your real estate desires, that I think I can get across today.

If you want to, look at the titans of the industry...whether the real estate industry, the high tech industry, etc. Back at the turn of the century – the industrial age – those innovators were not afraid to take risks. You're going to have regrets in life. We all *want* to live a life with no regrets – I do, you do, everybody reading wants to live a life with no regrets, but it's just not going to be the case. We will have them, but I want to go down regretting what I did do not what I didn't do.

When I'm sitting on that porch in a rocking chair 50 years from now, if I'm going to regret anything, I regret building that $125 million house because it took forever to sell. But, you know what? I did it! I tried it! I never want to sit in that rocking chair saying that I regret something that I didn't do.

That is so key. That book again, Frank...if you could just share that again. What's the name and author of that book?

Go to my website www.Frank-McKinney.com and click on "about Frank McKinney". There's

"Frank's Top 10 Reading List", and, under that list, there are a number of books – actually, I think three of them were written by Anthony De Mello... he's a great philosopher.

I'm reading a lot of philosophy books now. I've moved from reading the how-to books to now reading books either on philosophy or books written by do-ers – somebody who can really walk their talk.

My top 10 reading list contains a summary of each book that I've read, and why I think it would be a really good read for anybody, not just real estate people. So, spend some time on that site and take a look at those books. Then go out and get them. That's the way I educate myself is I am constantly reading books like that.

Me too...non-stop. Sometimes you just start asking yourself questions that someone has already answered for you. So, you're not alone. I read every day, for at least an hour, on people that are do-ers, not just talkers. By doing that, it relaxes me and gives me confidence in what I'm doing. I don't want to say it eliminates them, but it definitely conquers a lot of my fears that I face on a daily basis. If I'm trying to do something bigger, trying to take the next step to kick it up a notch, reading books like that helps build my risk muscle on a daily basis.

I commend you because one of the things we can never stop doing is learning. When you get to a certain level, you kind of think that you know a lot. When the moment comes, that's the moment you start losing ground to your competitor.

I'll never forget two years when I went to

meet with Donald Trump in his office. I had like a half-hour meeting with him, and I was going to have him endorse my second book. A couple of the topics we were going to discuss...and I had gone in with a list of questions prepared to ask him because, hey, I wanted to learn some things. This was my time to be mentored by somebody that I looked up to.

Well, it didn't work out that way, Mark. For 25 of the 30 minutes, he was hammering me with questions about the high-end, speculative single family real estate market, which is something, at the time, he'd never gotten into. He'd never built single family detached speculative homes.

So, now look at what he's doing...we're actually competing against each other! He's doing another nine-figure house up in Palm Beach. It's a renovation and a spec house. I came away with only having one or two of my questions answered, but I also came away with the fact that, "Oh my gosh, here's a guy who's never finished. He's never satisfied with his learning curve and is constantly educating himself." That is the lead I will take and continue to take and so should everybody reading this.

Absolutely — it's continuous growth that doesn't stop just because you start seeing success. I was talking to my mentor yesterday about this. He's like, "'Mark, we all have coaches." Let's take a professional football player, for instance. If they make it into the Super Bowl, that's as high as you can go in the football world. But, they don't fire the coach after that and try to do it themselves the next year — they will always need a coach because that's how they got there in the first place.

43

You've got to always stay around that positive mental attitude – the one that keeps you moving forward. You've got to keep up to date with what's going on in your marketplace. You've got to keep up to date with any new resources available to you, and you've always got to be improving upon your skillset. It's key, and, like you said, Frank, successful people are always asking questions. How can I do this? How can I make it better? Etc.

Just remember that very, very few people internally generate what I call "Vitamin M". The "M" stands for motivation. We need to get it from outside sources. I prefer to get it from somebody who can walk their talk.

I can't stand listening to a "guru" for the sake of somebody being a "guru". I think it's kind of screwed up the real estate educational industry since there are "gurus" out there that just prey on people's "hunger" and the fact that maybe they're not satisfied with where they are with their life, so they're looking for a better way. I question a lot of those guys. When was the last time they did a deal? Show me. Are they out there everyday with their "lunch pail" and "bringing it" like I have for 20 years?

I agree 100%, Frank. There are too many people out there trying to sell information that know nothing about the real estate industry.

It took me that long to get to where I am, and now I want to share it with others...and why shouldn't I? It's kind of a responsibility that I have to do what we're doing, even today with this

44

interview. If I can save somebody time, money and aggravation when it comes to their learning curve of real estate with the knowledge that I have, that's a great thing.

I live with an abundance mentality, which means that there's always plenty to go around. There's very few things I know that I would call "Colonel Sanders Secrets"...things that I keep to myself, and that I don't share with other people.

That's what you're doing, Mark, and I think it's great. I think the programs that you have are good, and you must be providing results for those people that look up to you...and they pay you well for it. This isn't something that you offer for free...you make a living at it, and you should.

The proof is in the pudding. There's a reason, folks, that when you get an email from Mark Evans or you go to his website, he doesn't have a DR next to his name...he's got a DM. That's a very special privilege because that stands for "Deal Maker". Mark Evans, The Master Deal Maker!

That's right! Thanks, Frank! The thing is, we still do deals too, not just talk about it. I walk my talk. I can do deals all day long — that's not even the question — but I do think that my deals get better as I help more people do their own deals. I want to make it easier for them, which ends up making it easier for me.

Having that driving force behind me to make it smoother for them is what keeps me going... making it more understandable, making it easier, etc. I tell everybody that comes to me and is who dedicated to the process that it will happen for them, no matter what...but only if they stick with

45

it.

The dedication to the longevity of it, like you said, is so key. The "get rich quick"...that's just bologna. I'm dedicated to the process — to do what ever it takes to get where I want to go. And those levels change as I grow too because some of the stuff I haven't even dreamed up yet. So, as I'm continuously growing, things start changing, and — literally — reaching whatever my next goal is almost happens with ease now.

That's great. As young as you are to make that statement...you've got a bright future ahead of you.

Thank you. On to that point, Frank. In your book, *Frank McKinney's Maverick Approach To Real Estate Success*, on page 234 you talk about when that $50 million house sold, and you fell to your knees in your tree house. Could you talk about that a little bit, and just explain that this is why you're at where you're at now? But it's just never-ending because it's instilled in us to continuously keep busy moving forward.

I've done a lot of interviews, and that is one question I've never had a chance to answer unless I was talking in front of a group and brought it up myself. I'm glad you did because that page in the book was another very big epiphany moment for me.

And, again, my second book, *Frank McKinney's Maverick Approach To Real Estate Success How You Can Go from a $50,000 Fixer-Upper to a $100 Million Mansion*, takes the reader on a journey that begins with that first

46

$50,000 fixer-upper all the way through to now where we are building $100+ million houses. It's a fascinating read if you chose to kind of take that journey with me. Or, "get on the bus" to the $50,000 fixer-upper if you don't have to desire to get off at building the $100 million mansion... there are plenty of stops along the way and many ways to make money. Don't feel like you've got to read this and then go out and get to a $100 million property...that's not the point. The point is to get on the bus at $50,000 or whatever you're entry-level home is.

And I really think people *should* start out where they are comfortable at and then start working their way up by building their "risk muscle".

That's correct. For years and years, subconsciously, I had this notion that life was, or my career was, about the end-game. That it was all about getting to a certain point or a certain net worth where things were going to be easy. It was a lot of time spent in "pursuit mode" rather than enjoying the ride.

That became really clear to me the day, as you referenced in the book a minute ago, we had just finished (this was last year, in 2005) selling a $7 million "spec" house, a $17 million "spec" house, and a $50 million "spec" house in a span of less than two months. Now, it took a long time to create those and all that, but they closed, ironically, very quickly.

As that last wire transfer came in – the $50 million was the last transaction to close – I'll never forget it. I'm talking to you today from my

47

tree house, and this is where everything happens. I have this beautiful tree house that overlooks the Atlantic Ocean where I design my houses and write my books from. But, I was sitting here on the same phone when my banker called and said, "Frank the wire hit."

That must have been an amazing feeling.

I'll never forget dropping to my knees, putting my hands over my face, putting my face down with my forehead on the floor of my office and just sobbing. It was uncontrollable, and it was something that was pretty unconscious...the whole act.

I said to myself, "It's over, it's over, it's over." What I realized after that whole thing happened ...maybe six months later – was that we need to be careful about setting end goals. It's the journey that counts. The part about arriving – the struggle and the strife, the ups and the downs. Getting there is when I felt most alive.

I've heard and read about so many successful people doing and saying the exact same thing.

Six months after those deals closed, what I realized was – and I know we talk about it in that chapter – is that money provides two things, relief and comfort. It does not provide happiness. I've met my fair share of unhappy billionaires, and I've met more than my fair share of very happy homeless people. I deal with both of them on a daily basis. I learn a lot from both of them on a daily basis.

Yes, the goal of buying your first property

48

or making your first $10,000 on a deal or whatever it is...those are great goals but be careful saying "end goal". Like, "When I make $1 million I'm going to retire" or "When I sell my one-hundredth property I'm going to retire" or "When I have one hundred rentals I'm going to retire". And, especially if you're pretty young, that is a really dangerous thing to do.

It definitely is. Like I said, as I grow, success is achieved at different levels. There's no way I ever dreamed of being where I am today — and now I keep setting higher goals for the future.

It's just so funny to me now because, back then, my end goal would have been to be able to do what I want, when I want. Now that I can do that, it's...I think you used the word "euphoria".

One of the misconceptions, I think, is, "Ok, this guy's a millionaire, and he's living in a huge mansion, driving exotic cars, and doing all this stuff — he must be 'done'." What I've seen in the past, with people I surround myself with, is that they're all do-ers and are never 'done'.

Not only that, but they learn more than the people that aren't doing anything or making that much money. We're constantly educating ourselves and learning from what we do and what those around us are doing.

A great example. You all are in this business. But, especially for those of you who are younger, it's hard to hear what I'm going to say. You all dream about winning the lottery, and many people take a "winning lottery approach" to real estate investing.

There are books and articles out there

49

about lottery winners. Over 90% of them either go broke, are highly medicated because of their depression, commit suicide or end up in jail because of that instant change in lifestyle like you just referenced – "I want to do what I want when I want".

You're in your twenties, so that's what you should be saying. But, when you get to do that at such a young age...well, what's left? If that's all you want to do – not you Mark, but anybody reading – then you're going to live a pretty shallow life. You're going to find depression, even though you've got a ton of money in the bank. I've seen it with some of the people I sell these high-end houses to, and it's a really sad thing.

If you've got a greater call...and, for me, it's my caring House Project Foundation...that's what's going to get you up in the morning. It really and truly does. That's when I stop wondering why I'm working so hard when I don't need to anymore.

To me, I found a great dovetailing, if you will, between my spiritual highest calling and my professional highest calling. Isn't that wonderful? Isn't that what we all strive to do? Kind of like Bill Gates...he had a great professional calling by inventing software. Now, though, his Bill and Melinda Gates Foundation is the world's largest foundation – over $29 billion.

Imagine the impact he could have on the world with those kind of resources, and his application of those resources. To me, that's what it's all about. And I don't know the average age of your readers, but I know...Mark, you're like 26, 27 right?

I'll be 28 on Monday.

My birthday is pretty close to yours, actually ...mine's June 28th. So, I'm 14 years older than you, and you're succeeding at such a higher level than I was 14 years ago. If you don't set yourself up for this future of sharing something's God has given you, it's going to be shallow, and it's going to be empty.

The consumables in our lives...let's face it, you can only eat so much, wear so many clothes, have so many cars in your garage, have so many planes in your hangar, and, if you really "get there", so many yachts in your marina, so many sports teams, etc. I learned that from Rich DeVoss, who is one of my mentors. He said, "Frank how many consumables do you really need?" The answer is that you really *don't* need them.

Once you get your basic needs met, then what are you going to do with the other resources? You're going to share them with those that don't have any. That's the best! That's what makes me tick is a lot of people that I look up to...it makes life really worth living.

Absolutely, Frank. I must admit something. I didn't sleep a wink last night because I was so excited to talk to you and told everybody about it. Because when it's someone you look up to, and now you have the privilege to talk to him on this level...it's amazing.

I know when we were on the book tour bus with you earlier this year, and we stopped in little stores in small towns, I was blown away by just your dedication to touch the people's lives. To get your book in front of people, on your part, is just so key and big, and, obviously, that's why you're

51

taking the Maverick Approach — making it big everyday, even in the little things.

It's all about the process. You're so committed to it, which I admire, and those are the things that I look up to as I grow because all that "stuff" is...well, I don't need all that "stuff" anymore. That's what I thought I needed because I didn't know any better. But, as I started to progress and look up to the right people, my perspective on all that changed.

Doug was on the bus with us too, and he and I spoke about it afterwards. We were like, "This guy...why is he doing this? He doesn't need to do this, but he's out here doing it anyway." I know that made a huge impact on everything that you set yourself up to do, and I just thought that was an awesome opportunity for Doug and I...just to experience it.

I would never tell anybody reading this to, as an evangelist would say, "touch the book and you will be healed". I'm no angel, and I don't live this perfect prized-like life, but, at the same time, I understand this business. I'm going to quote a little scripture, if you don't mind? A passage in the Bible from Luke. To paraphrase, it says, "To whom much is entrusted, much will be expected. To whom more is entrusted, more will be expected." You may not think that you've been entrusted with a lot, but you know what? You have. You've been entrusted with the three T's — time, talent and treasure. Maybe not so much treasure, and maybe not so much talent, in the beginning. But, we all have time to share with those less fortunate.

For me, it started over ten years ago by

serv ing hot meals just once a week – every Monday night – to homeless people from the back of a beat-up old Econoline van...a rusty, old Econoline van. That was sharing the first "T", the only "T" I had at the time, and that was time.

I bet a lot of people reading this only have that "T" right now too.

Back then, I had a little talent. I had a real estate company...I had a construction company, and we went out to where people lived to feed them because they were incapable of doing it for themselves due to being older or handicapped. We did a few of those and felt good about it, and I know the people were happy about it.

Then, it came time for me to share my treasure. I stopped feeding the homeless myself because I knew I could do more, and I stopped having my own crew go out there and renovate houses. We now are doing a HUGE village over in Haiti right now that will affect over 500 people in the city we're building in. We're building a whole, self-sufficient village that combines an orphanage, pool, a community center, houses, a clinic for sick, a renewable food source and clean drinking water. Seven elements all combined in this village.

That is just so amazing, Frank.

It took me a long time, Mark. It took me a long time to understand that passage "to whom much is trusted, much will be expected." I was reading an article today online about Bill Gates' retirement. He basically, without quoting the scripture, said that "with great wealth comes

53

great responsibility".

My third book that I'm working on is one that I'm sure not a lot real estate people are going to read. It's based around a premise that I believe, which is that God hands people things to use to succeed – and that's very controversial, so a lot of people aren't going to like it.

Frank, I couldn't agree with you more. I look forward to reading that book.

Now that we're on this subject, with the kind of wealth that you've been exposed to, how have you seen people handle that abundance of wealth?

I have seen in my life that those that know how to handle abundance, know how to handle wealth, in a responsible manner are the ones that continue to succeed. You might have the flash-in-the-pan variety...and I'm not ripping on rock stars or rappers, but guys who make a bunch of money...boat loads of money – well, maybe a lot of them are very charitable, but I'm not so sure. If they aren't, it will definitely show up later on in their lives. But, if they understand the responsibility and the stewardship that comes along with those blessings, then that's the kind of legacy that lasts forever!

I know we're getting off track here, and we want to talk about real estate, but you are good enough to be able to teach your people how to make money. I have no doubt about that. If you apply what Mark tells you, then you're going to do fine. If you take a long-term approach, you're going to make money. I'm just saying please think beyond that act of taking the check.

54

That is huge — the big picture — and it IS what I strive for everyday. How can I improve what I'm doing to change someone's life? How can I improve my teaching techniques to get people to the next level faster? That is the stuff that is on my mind more than cashing checks.

My real estate business is not just about real estate. My approach to my real estate business is as a "people person" business. If people don't like you, you're not going to do deals. Houses don't make decisions, people do.

You're absolutely right. That's one of my favorite chapters in my second book..."thank people first, and then profit will follow."

It's so key, but everybody's out there going, "I need a deal...I need a deal" No. Step away from it, and focus on the people. What are their fears? What are they feeling? Where are they at? What's going on in their life?

We all face different challenges every single day, and if you're going after foreclosures or tired landlords or whatever it may be, these people are in a situation that they don't want to be in anymore. Just be out there and really see who these guys are and understand where they're coming from. It's the first step I took, and that's why we continue to be successful because we really do care about the people...it's not just the profits.

Frank, I also wanted to talk about the fact that you know that you couldn't do all the things you do by yourself, so could you talk a little bit about how Frank McKinney sets up his team, and

how key it's been to your success?

Again, this won't be anything too new, but I think the first thing you need to recognize when you set up your structure is to identify your weaknesses. Identify what you aren't good at or that you know others can do better than you. Your strengths are going to be obvious to yourself and to others – they're going to be easy...that's why they're called your strengths.

Early on I had a ton of weaknesses – a big one was lack of education. There was no real estate in my family. My father was a banker, and my mother was a school teacher. I have five brothers and sisters, and none of them got involved in real estate, except for my younger brother, who got into it after me. So, I realized my goodness. Even to this day I'm not the best at reading plans. I'm a very visual person, a very three-dimensional person, verses being a two-dimensional person.

Through my experience, I've read about a lot of ultra-successful people being this way. That is why having a team that is good where you're not so good is key.

In the real estate business, though, the most important thing to remember is to keep your team small. Most people think that to set up a business in the proper way, you need a ton of overhead, a fancy office, and all these employees. That's just not the case. I have a HUGE company, but right now I have only five employees.

I agree...I have a very small team in place.

When we get into a big project, like this one, we're very top-heavy when it comes to overhead. I'm hiring my own general contractor, even though, up until this point, we have been our own general contractor. This project is just way too large for me to do...it's 67,672 square feet. There's no way I want to tackle this by myself, so I've hired a general contractor. I'm even hiring an owner's representative, and I've never done that before. But, this contractor is a guy who's built a couple 70,000 square foot houses as an owner's rep, not as a contractor, and he's worked for other high net-worth individuals as an owner's rep. Even though I'm not the owner, of course, as in putting my head on the pillow, I do own the property until I sell it.

The engineers that I have around me are top notch architects, structural, civil, mechanical and coastal engineers (because we're building on the ocean). I'm surrounded by people that do their jobs way better than I ever could. I'm just kind of the ring leader. I get them together, we hire them, we negotiate their contracts, etc. My personal assistant, Mark, who you met on the bus, Mark...he's a great right-hand man.

All these people are supportive of the Frank McKinney way. We talk about that in the second book – how you identify a culture in your company and encourage your employees to live that culture. It is a lifestyle, and if they don't live it, then they don't stay. It's that simple.

I run my business the same way and had to let people go who weren't on-board for the long run.

I'm a firm believer in the approach that Jack Welch, the CEO of General Electric uses. He says that, "The bottom 10% of your company are the ones that are always bringing the other 90% down." So, he's constantly ridding himself of the bottom 10%. Every company has it, but it's harder the smaller you are. If you start out with 100 people in your company, it's really easy to get rid of 10. But when you have 10, and you have to get rid of 1...that's tough. It's really hard, but that's the way to keep that culture fresh.

It is really hard to do sometimes, but you always know, later, that it was the best thing.

And, people, we're talking with a lot of energy here. I'm doing better after 20 years, and I still have that same passion that I had with the first $50,000 fixer-upper. It's the people that I surround myself with that do their jobs better than I do. Because I've identified my weaknesses and brought those on who will compliment them, that has caused me to continue to stay passionate.

There's some daily stuff that Mark does. If I still had to do it, I don't think I'd like the business as much. But, because I don't want to do some of the daily stuff, it's that simple – I just don't want to do it. I'm not cut out to do some of it, so I've got somebody else that does it for me. But, if it had taken me a long time to identify that I wasn't good at it or didn't want to do it anymore, I may have burned out. So, surround yourself with that great team from the start.

I know that's what we've done. At one time, Frank, I was that guy that thought you had

to have the big, fancy office and all that stuff and do it all myself to be successful. I call that my "million dollar mistake" because I thought that's what people needed to see to do business with me. Actually, it was the total opposite because it was so out of character for me that I actually did _less_ business when I had the big office.

When it was just me again, with my small team in place, doing what I do, things just started falling together again because I was living to my fullest potential...I wasn't trying to be something I wasn't.

It's a lot more enjoyable too. I was starting to get burned out because I was in that office micro-managing all of the day to day stuff, and nothing was getting done, on my part.

I commend you for recognizing that so early. It's usually something where you hit a burn out point, and then it's too late. But, you've recognized it and...heck, I work out of a tree house for God's sake. I don't have anybody else around me. I have a main office that's a half a mile away, where I work. I go over there maybe once every two weeks or so. Mark and I meet here. My projects are on A1A – that road is right out in front of my tree house!

I think it's imperative to surround yourself with an environment that is conducive to creativity and productivity. When I sit down and design a 67,672 square foot house, you better believe my thumbprint...not my handprint but my thumbprint ...is on every square inch of that 67,672 square feet. I need an environment that's conducive to creating something like that. When I wrote my two books...I was very bored in English class in

59

school...obviously, with a 1.8 grade point average ...but I love to write. I need an environment that can bring out the best in my writings.

That's really important for anybody who's getting into a business like real estate, where creativity is a very important part. Why? Because you've got a lot of competition. If you're not creative in your design, in your renovation, in how you furnish your houses, in how you accessories them, in how you merchandise them, in how you market them, in how you sell them, in how you build your brand, then you're just like every other investor out there.

We're very keen on brand-building. We're very, very keen on what the "it" is that sets apart the Frank McKinney artistry from every other house out there. That's it...that word "artistry". We build "artwork" that you live in. We create artwork that you enjoy rather than just sit back and look at on a wall. So the other side of the lesson is making sure your working environment is conducive to drawing out the creativity that sets your "brand" apart.

Absolutely. Frank, while we are on this, could you talk for a minute about how key that is for this house you're now creating and building? What kind of buyers — how many buyers — will be able to buy it? How tight is your niche, I guess, in this industry? Could you go into that a little bit because it's just mind-blowing to me how strong your risk muscle is knowing that this number is so small.

It starts with recognizing that — and we just finished talking about creativity and artistry

60

and all that wonderful stuff – it still starts out with recognizing that you must be a businessman first. But, yes, what we create is artwork.

I'm building a pool with an acrylic wall and a shark tank, so that if you go down the slide you slide over the sharks...fall into the pool, and it appears as if you're swimming around with the sharks. The master bedroom in this house is over 6,000 square feet. The list of "wow factors" goes on and on and on in this house.

But, if it didn't make business sense, I wouldn't do it. There are a lot of starving artists out there, and I ain't gonna be one. So, we did a tremendous amount of market research when it came to answering the question, "Who could buy this house?"

And, as a businessman, it is one of the most important factors that you must know.

If you have an opportunity to combine your artistry and your creativity with the business side, then you've got "one leg up" because, most often, you will find someone who is very strong in their business sense and very weak in their creative sense or vice versa. I'm pretty good at both.

We went out and determined that there were about 8,000 people in the world that had a net worth that would allow for them the opportunity to buy a house of over nine figures. We also determined that there was very little competition out there going after those 8,000 people, although there was some, and that's good...I'm not so sure I would be doing this if I was the only one. So, yes, I'm a risk-taker, but, hey, I don't want to be the only "white elephant".

61

I don't want to build a billion-dollar house in a $300,000 neighborhood. I'm just not going to be that stupid.

Of course not.

So, we identified that there's 8,000 people, and probably 1% of those 8,000 (80 people) might be what I call "subliminally looking" for the perfect, ultra-high-end home. I say "subliminally" because they're not in their car driving around looking for it. But, if it were to hit them at the right moment, and in the right fashion, they would come down and consider buying it.

So, if there's about 80 people out of a worldwide population of six and a half billion that could buy this, we still have trouble convincing the bankers that this is a great investment. But, at the same time, if there are 80 people out there that might be in the market for a house of this size and of this price point, there's only three or four people like me going after them. Only three or four *properties* going after them. So, I like my chances, and I've always used that analogy.

And, by now, you've shown your banker enough times that your properties will sell, so that's gotta help some.

Yes, but still, I can't tell you how many times I've been asked, "Frank, my goodness. A $30 million house? How many people can afford it?" The answer is about 50,000 — 50,000 out of six and a half billion, so your chances are pretty slim. If you look at it in those terms, then, yes, it's a bit of a scary investment. But, how many — out

62

of those 50,000 people – how many houses like mine are there out there going after those 50,000 people? The answer is "very few". And, I usually know how many, and where they are.

So, there's a tremendous amount of market research that goes into it. Then, it all kind of clashes like the splitting of an atom and just comes together. What has to happen when that atom splits? Does it make sense in the marketplace? Can you be as creative as possible building this wonderful piece of art? Can you market it properly? Can you balance what I call the "Holy Trinity" – which is time, budget and quality – when you go into a project like this? And the answer – if you could answer all of those questions in the affirmative and get over the fear that, believe me, I wrestle with – then the answer's going to be, "Yes, let's do it."

Frank, on something like that...on the $30 million house. How does that work? What do you do to get it sold? Can you talk to our readers about the five senses and how you take the buyers on that journey through the property with all five of their senses being heightened? Can you talk to us about the guy that just purchased your property ...and he didn't even know that he was looking to buy! Talk about how all that happened due to the five senses.

So, you're talking about how we get people to buy what we build?

Yes, with the five senses approach. I know that when I was fortunate enough to go through your $17 million house, I walked in and I was just

**in awe. All of my senses were just urging me...
I wanted to buy it! There's just this power that
takes over your body when you walk into one of
your pieces of art.**

The "Most Important Marketing Lesson" is
the longest chapter in the second book. Basically,
the second book teaches you and shows you how
to locate, negotiate, buy, improve, market and
sell these properties. Whether it be a $50,000
house or a $50 million house. The "Market and
Sell" chapter is the longest chapter out of the 280
or so pages that the whole book is.

When it comes to marketing and selling,
regardless of price point, the most important thing
you should look to accomplish is to heighten your
buyer's five senses. The experience your buyer
is having with his or her five senses should lead
them to the state of subliminal euphoria – to the
intoxicating state of subliminal euphoria.

You have somebody's attention for an
hour, depending on the size of the house. So, you
have one hour in which to excite their sense of
sound, smell, see, touch and taste to a level that
makes the buyer feel euphoric. What he thinks
what he's perceiving is unlike anything else he's
seen before.

What he's smelling in terms of beautiful
ocean breezes that might be blowing through
the windows one day or the seasonal, scented
potpourri that my wife puts throughout. From the
plants inside the house to the cookies in the oven
of your $50,000 fixer-upper with the oven turned
to 125 degrees instead of 425 degrees...that's a
nice smell walking through the house.

I've done this so many times, with the cookies, and recommend for my students to do it too...it really works.

It sure does. Touching. I have a rule that you've got to take off your shoes when you come to one of my houses. Yes, I want to keep them clean, but I also want you to feel the $200 per square yard carpet that we put in the master bedroom, that's four and a half inches thick. You put your foot on that...I had a billionaire once say to me, "Frank I wouldn't need a mattress." They wouldn't perceive that with their shoes on. Tell them to go over and touch the velvet on the walls in the theater or the leather on the walls in the office.

Taste. In the early days, I put out Doritos and Coke, not just because I wanted to have something for them to eat, but it was more for the conversational aspect. The reason for this is to keep the person in the house a little longer so that I can express what I had in mind when I created this piece of art.

And you need to *look* at your houses as art. I don't care if they're crack houses in a bad part of town. They're art — it's your form of art. It's not just this box that's an investment for you. It is art, no matter what.

Now-a-days, we have butlers and people that serve caviar and champagne. If you come to one of our houses, you're treated very well when it comes to what you're going to eat, with chocolates and all.

You really spoil people when they come through.

Yes, that's the point. Sound. We put in sound systems that are $200,000+ sound systems with speakers that are hidden behind drywall that allows the sound to permeate, but you can't see the source of the sound. I put speakers under water. On a nice day, I might turn everything off and let the crashing waves kind of permeate through the house.

You really need to read that chapter again because there are dozens of examples of we have used over the years to cause a potential buyer's senses to be heightened to the state of "subliminal euphoria" – you get them to that point.

It's all about being creative and doing what no one else is doing.

Yes. In any situation, you want to move your potential buyer from need to desire. Now at your entry level home – whatever price point that may be for where you live – those buyers are driven by need. I need to put a roof over my head – therefore, I'm going to look at Mark Evans' house. When you can take that need, fill it and then turn it into a desire...make them desire your house.

It's like Mark walking down the center of the mall and wanting to buy a new jacket. He has a nice looking jacket on already, but the moment he sees the "right" jacket through the storefront window, he's going to go buy it because the retailer did a nice job of moving his need for the jacket to a desire to have it.

Absolutely...I can't count how many times

that   has happened to me, Frank.

So, the more expensive the home, the less the need will be. This level of buyer doesn't need to put a roof over their head. Believe me, that need is long taken care of – this is a desirous purchase. Just like I desire to go out and buy a new tennis racket or a new car, I'm desirous of that purchase, not in "need" of it. The retailer/seller has done a good job of "finding" my five senses with that "subliminal euphoria", and I buy it.

So, I encourage you to re-read that chapter. If you don't want to re-read the chapter again, then take a yellow piece of paper and write down the five senses, and write down what you can do to heighten those five senses to that state of "subliminal euphoria" and then go do it.

This is great stuff. Well, Frank, I definitely want to touch on the Caring House Project Foundation as well as make sure the readers know what they can do to help you keep the Caring House Project Foundation going strong...to give that extra little bit, or whatever they can, to make some peoples' dreams come true through the Caring House Project Foundation. Can you repeat your website address?

Just go to www.Frank-McKinney.com, and there's a tool bar at the top where you can click on the Caring House Project Foundation. You can read about what we've done, and what we're doing now. I think what's great about our Foundation – and what people appreciate – is that you know right away that...let's say that Mark

67

donated $4,000 to ride with us on the bus, well, he built a house. For $4,000, Mark built a house in Haiti that will house eight homeless people – a family of eight.

If you can't do $4,000, which is a huge amount of money, $25 buys the hardware to a front door, $100 will buy the windows, $500 buys the concrete. You can see all of this broken down on our website. It's amazing how far our money goes in these countries that are so desperately poor.

A great analogy is that what I do for a living costs about $1,000 per square foot, like I just described with our beautiful, oceanfront mansion. The average house in America, Mark, averages just a little over $41 per square foot. So, what I can do for $10 per square foot...with $4,000... is build a whole house out of concrete. Concrete foundation and walls, a metal roof, two rooms, a kitchen, front porch and a separate house for going to the bathroom and showering. Again, all out of concrete – and that includes the land, the clearing of the land...everything! That's amazing!

I still can't believe that only $4,000 builds an entire house!

I know. Go to the website, and you can see how you can impact, whatever the size of your donation is, a family and know that your money is being put to work immediately.

The other thing that's really great is that we don't have the overhead that most Foundations have. Because of my speculative approach to real estate I take the same approach to our Foundation ...I run it like a business. The only difference is that there's no profit or profit motive in terms of a personal profit motive.

Yes, I want to profit for the people that we can touch with those profits, but we operate on about a 5% expense overhead ratio. Nobody draws a salary – I don't, Mark doesn't, Lori doesn't, Nilsa doesn't, Martha doesn't. Anybody that works for us, works for no salary. We might have to buy some pens and paperclips, little things like that, but, for the most part, all the money received goes into what we do.

That's awesome...there's not a lot of charities out there can say that.

If you want to buy a book from me, for example, on our website, the profit mechanism is the Caring House Project Foundation. The book isn't bought from Frank and Frank writes the check that goes to the Foundation. The credit card is processed by the Caring House Project Foundation.

You can buy a book for $25 and know that the $25 went to small villages over there. I'm not shameful at all about asking for donations for what we do because what we do costs a lot of money. The more I can bring in, the more I can do for these people. In my lifetime, Mark, in the grand scheme of things, I won't make that big of an impact over in Haiti, but I do all I can.

There is a great quote from Mother Teresa that I keep next to my desk. It says, "What we are doing is just a drop in the ocean, but the ocean would be less because of that missing drop." That's the way I look at it. Will I make a huge impact over there? No, but the impact we're making on, say, 500 lives, is great, and it's immediate, and it's leaving it better than I found it.

That's what I want people to feel good about – knowing that they're helping to make this happen. If you go buy a book or...I also have a series that I created up here in the tree house, an audio series that I recorded on this digital recording equipment across from my desk. I set one of my seven-year-old daughter's little dolls up, and I imagined that I was talking to that very person who was listening to that series. Not reading a bedtime story like some of these audio series' are where the guy just reads what's in the book, I'm actually pre-associating, like we're doing right now, not reading from any scripts at all.

Ah, Frank...we need to tell them about the action figure...

Oh, yeah...there's a little action figure – a talking action figure. It's laughable, it's hilarious, and it's not even to be taken seriously. All the proceeds from those sales went to our Caring House Project Foundation.

I would love for your listeners to take *your* lead, not mine, and donate to our Foundation. Real charity doesn't know what "tax deductible" means, and when I say "real charity", you're doing this to help people, not for the deduction, but you do get a tax deduction. The impact that you can make is unbelievable. As soon as it's safe over there, and it's getting safer, I'm bringing you, and some other people that donated a lot of money, over there, and then you will then be a disciple. Once you come home, you will be out there trying to make more money to do more.

Awesome. That's going to be an exciting experience. I do look forward to that. And, Frank, I really do appreciate you taking the time to talk to me today. I know how busy you are, so thank you.

Like I said, just being around you has changed the way I take my Maverick Approach to my real estate – and not just real estate but in my life as well.

I'm going to continuously support the Caring House Project Foundation because it's such a great benefit to so many people.

Let's give your website address one more time...it's <u>www.Frank-McKinney.com.</u> Go there and go through the whole thing...it's an awesome website. There's a lot of great stuff to check out.

Thank you, Mark. I want to see you "Make It Big" and be a "Maverick" and continue to share your blessings.

Excellent. Thank you Frank. Have a great day.

Bye.

"Strength does not come from winning. Your struggles develop your strengths. When you go through hardships and decide not to surrender, that is strength."

**- Arnold Schwarzenegger;
Actor / Governor of California**

"Have the courage to say no. Have the courage to face the truth. Do the right thing because it is right. These are the magic keys to living your life with integrity."

- W. Clement Stone

Chapter Three
Interview with TC Bradley

What you're about to read is a very powerful interview. The guy on the other line has done a lot for me and helped me to grow in many different ways in a very short period of time. I'm so excited to have him here — it's a privilege and an honor. Both he and his wife are just great people to be around.

I want to start it off by introducing him and getting the ball rolling so that we can maximize the time we have and get you some great information that will help you get to the next level.

TC, are you there?

Yes, I am, Mark.

Everyone, this is TC Bradley. Like I said, he has done a lot for me and many others out there. I've had the privilege of sitting down with him and just hanging out with him. He definitely knows his stuff, and that's why I'm interviewing him now.

You want to take it from there, TC, and give a little background on yourself to get us going?

Sure. Mark, thank you for the invitation to come here and speak. I certainly do appreciate it. Before I do that, I want to honor you, of course. I think that you're absolutely fantastic and phenomenal. I think that you've got some brilliant marketing concepts. You blow me away with the

73

things that you're doing, so it is a privilege and an honor to be here for me too.

Excellent, thank you.

So, what would you like me to cover...a little bit of background?

Yes. The whole theme for this interview tonight, and what we really want to stick to, is the importance of getting that first deal done. So many times I have talked to great people who are very intelligent, and they have a lot of information and knowledge, but I think the biggest key is... and what I want to focus on...is that it all starts with the first deal...how truly important that first deal really is.

It's not about focusing on a hundred deals a month or whatever you're shooting for right now. So many people get caught up in the big numbers, TC. I just want to really stick to that first one, and show everyone how powerful it is and what it can/will do for your life.

I firmly believe, Mark, that one real estate deal can change your entire life forever. I do want to preface this interview tonight by letting people know that I've really, really been marinating on this interview and on the people that I know will be reading it, and I really do believe that tonight could be a defining moment in somebody's life simply by taking in all that we're about to talk about.

I've had defining moments in my life, and one of them happened January the 8th of 2001 when our partner terminated our partnership and told us that he was going to be kind enough to keep our multi-million dollar company that we had started just six months earlier. In a moment...in a twinkling of an eye...my whole life had turned upside down.

That is just awful...what some people will do for a buck. Did you have any idea of what you were going to do next?

It was a defining moment in my life, and I can tell you that I was faced with a choice of doing something. I had to do something to put money in my account that month. Now, being down here in Florida, you just can't go and get a J-O-B to replace the type of income that I was used to making at the time.

I can remember my wife looking at me and saying to me – she was ash and gray – she said to me, "What are we going to do?" Without hesitation and without blinking an eye, I said, "We're going to invest in real estate."

You see, Mark, I told you earlier how Vickie and I had sort of backed into this thing the opposite way. I didn't do this the way that normal people get involved in real estate.

Wow...you weren't kidding! But it's that kind of quick decision-making that creates successful people, such as yourself.

It's kind of an interesting story. We first used what we now teach to secure our dream house here in Florida...all without a credit check. We have a beautiful home here in Florida that we've been blessed with – we're on the water, it's a beautiful home, and we got it without a credit check.

Now, I'm not going to get into all the people that told me that I couldn't do what I was going to do. We won't get into that topic. But, I want you to know that if you're reading this, and all you ever want to do is secure your dream house, well I've been to that Bar-B-Que.

You see, my whole mantra was that I wanted to build a business. I wasn't going to be a full time investor. But, then the carpet got pulled out from underneath me in a moment, and it happens everyday in our society, Mark.

Unfortunately, that is true, so being in complete control of your financial future is key. I mean, for you it was a company that got taken away, which is a lot to lose, but most people would be devastated if they lost their job tomorrow.

Somebody reading this, as a matter of fact, may have gone to work today to a job that they thought was stable, and then they got a little notice with their paycheck that said, "Hey, your services are no longer required." A defining moment like that can change your life. That moment – on January the 8th of 2001 – was a defining moment in my life.

Ok, TC, let's get into it...let's talk about your first deal.

When you talk about the first deal, you talk about the first deal being the hardest deal. Without question, I can tell you, especially when you're under mounting pressure, how just hellacious that experience is. Now, once I drew the line in the sand and said this is what we're going to do... we're going to be full time real estate investors... well, then I went after it with a passion.

Now, understand we had done one deal, our own house, but that's not what I'm talking about at this moment in time. I'm talking about the first one that puts the 'doe-re-me' into your account...I'm talking about real money. I'm not talking about a buy and hold strategy where you buy something, hold onto it for five years and then you refinance it or you sell it and cash out. I had to do something to put money in my account *that* month. Every nickel we had was put into that company, Mark, every single nickel...and it was all taken from me in a moment.

You needed fast cash.

Yes. So, I went after this thing, but the first thing I did is was "let it go". I didn't have a pity party for myself, although I could have qualified for one very easily. I was not going to allow my ex-partner, "the skunk", to rob me of my future. I just went after real estate investing with a passion like never before. I had blinders on. I was focused. I was *going* to make it happen. Mark, my commitment level was this – I was going to do it or I was going to die...there was no in-between with me.

Good for you...it doesn't do any good anyway.

Of course not. When I hear people that come to me...well, there are two types. We have the people that come to us that were just in similar situations like we were just in and they have no choice *but* to make it. To me, those people are in the best position. Then, I have the people that come to me and say, "Well, TC, I want to try this. I want to get your material and I'm going to try this." I always tell them, Mark, to save their time and money, save both of our time, because "try" ain't going to get it *done*.

I can tell you, ladies and gentleman, that I do know what that feels like – to be in a position where you've got to make money NOW. And I didn't achieve my goals because I was the most talented or I was the sharpest crayon in the box. I just committed myself to getting it done.

It's all about persistence and consistent action...that will get you to where you want to go all day long more than just being book-smart.

You got it. Mark, that first deal that I got done because I *had* to...it took me two weeks to do. Now, you would think that that's not very much time, right? Well, it was the longest time for me because that first deal...it's like I always talk about the two fat men.

I tell this story to our students: there were two fat men that were sitting on each of my shoulders. The one fat man was whispering in my ear, "TC, you can do it. You know you can do it!" And then, at the same time, the other fat man had a hold of my other ear and was saying, "Who are you trying to kid? Who do you think you are? Who's going to give you their house without a credit check and $1 to $10 down?"

You see, that period of time between

78

committing to doing it, to two weeks later when I actually took down my first deal...well, I can tell you, Mark, that first deal was the hardest because it's mental. It was completely mental because all I could do was to do what I knew how to do. Does that make sense?

Absolutely. Most people get stopped in their tracks by that mental factor, but you have to push through it and have that belief in yourself...believe what the first "fat man" said instead (laughing).

And it just can't happen quick enough. You turn on the TV, and you see the infomercial. You go and surf online, and you see the testimonials. I have news for everybody reading this...all of the testimonials in the world don't mean a hill of beans until *you* do it. Then it becomes real. Then you become bulletproof.

But the problem, Mark, with people getting started in investing today...the challenge that they have is that they give up before they get that first deal.

I see it so many times...

I understand the agony because...and some people say, "TC, agony? Two weeks? Are you kidding me? That's not agony." But it was hellacious. Those days I was up from morning 'til night, and I was working this, and I was after it with a passion. And I have news for you...it was a long period of time for me.

You see, a lot of people get scared, nervous or anxious and they freeze up before they ever "pop" that first deal...but once they do...

Mark, if we could have people take a pill, a pill that pushes away the fears and the "I can't do it" mentality...*that* would keep them in the race and keep them focused until they got their first deal and then their life would be forever changed.

I'll bet we could sell a lot of *those* pills (laughing)!

You know it. And I'm not talking about the first deal having to be a whopper. I'm not talking about making tons of money on the first deal. If you only make $2,500 or $5,000 because you turned it around real quick...well, then you just put $5,000 in your account, and that's awesome.

The mere fact that you were able to do something that you didn't do before and now you know how to duplicate it. *That's* where the power is. The power is getting that first deal done. If I can stress anything, it would be to stress to people that we can give you the recipe for how to do this, but we can't give you the backbone.

And part of being successful is keeping that backbone through it all, even when it's hard.

I know what it's like because, you know, Mark, it's hard sometimes to understand, but I would say that the majority of people reading this might be working a full time job. They work all day, they fight traffic to and from, then they get home and woof down their dinner...the last thing they want to do is get on the phone and start working for deals. Especially when it ain't happening right away. But, that's exactly what you'll need to do to

80

succeed and have the life you want.

Exactly. I think you touched on a bunch of topics here, and I hope you readers have a pen and paper to write this stuff down because where TC is coming from, and where I'm coming from is that we've all been where you're at. It's just a part of the process.

With TC and the way he talks — with passion, persistence, dedication — these are big words that lead to success.

I see the same problem all the time, TC, when we're talking to people. They just want it all immediately. They don't want to do anything for it...they just want it to fall in their lap. Like you said, you can give them the recipe but you can't give them the backbone because they wouldn't appreciate it if you did anyway. It's so powerful, getting that first deal done, because now you're running full speed ahead with it.

Mark, everyone wants the first deal to go quickly. I wanted the first one to go quickly. The difference was that my commitment level was "come hell or high water, I'm taking that sucker down. I'm going to do it, and it doesn't matter to me whether it's the first call or the hundredth call...that bad boy is going down."

You see, *that* was the commitment. When you draw the line in the sand, when you become committed to something, the clouds will part, and you will receive divine providence. Then, everything will start moving forward from there. It doesn't move forward for the person that Mickey Mouse's around or who is half-heartedly committed to this and thinks to himself that "one day I'll do it, and then the next day I won't."

I wasn't half-hearted in what I did at all. If you think back to my story, I had no other choice. I had to do *something* to make real money that month in real estate. Often times, people will say that they're committed to doing something, but that doesn't always go very far.

I think the commitment to it is key. Like you said, you had no other alternative. We're not going around sticking our toe in the pond, we're getting it done. So many times, and I know you've heard this many times too, we get, "But how quick can you do a deal? I want to do a deal in one days or two days."

Well, we *can* do that. We understand the fundamentals and the pieces involved in putting a deal together. I can guarantee you that there are people reading this who I've personally told, "Look, you're not going to know anything until you do something. You're not going to know what kind of results you'll get. All of it is theory until you put it into action and apply it. That's when you can start to figure it out, and then it *will* start happening quickly...within two weeks or within thirty days or less."

I will say that we've had students that have come out of the box swinging, and I want to slap some of them...kidding, of course. People will say, "TC wanted to slap one of his students?!?!?!" No, I'm really proud of them because they were able to get a deal done within 48 hours, and it took me 2 weeks!

I'm just telling you that the possibility exists for anyone to come out of their own box like that. If you're taking notes, write this down, and I never want you to forget it! ***The better you get, the easier this gets.***

You see, everybody has to pay the price of success at the door. There are no discounts or free passes at the door of success. If you look at it, some of you may have already paid a tremendous price for your success, and you haven't even achieved it yet. But, you *have* paid the price of gaining knowledge and developing your skill set.

So, now you can come in, and you can get some information from Mark or myself, and then it clicks for you. The lightbulb now comes on and shines bright, and you get out there and you make it happen...and then things will happen for you – very quickly.

Somebody from a distance will look at you and say, "Wow, that guy is lucky." Luck had nothing to do with it. What they don't see is that you've already paid your price...you just paid it at a different bridge.

TC, I think you said something so powerful. You would do a deal – and I'm still the same way to this day – if it takes one call or one hundred calls. It doesn't matter, and, quite honestly, no one cares about that but us.

People only see what they see on the outside. They don't see what's going on in the house or in the office or wherever you're at when you're struggling to work it and make it happen and dealing with the things that come across your plate with real estate investing.

There are a lot of pieces that have to fall into place, and you've got to stay consistent for that to happen. I'll never forget one of my biggest

mentors that helped me a lot...if you're writing this down, this is another thing that stops a lot of people. It was a hard pill for me to swallow because I always wanted to do this...he said, "The reason most people fail is because they're trying to do it right. You don't have to get it right, you just have to get it going." When you get it going, I promise you, things will start to happen.

Mark, people think it's a journey of a thousand steps, and you *do* have to strive towards what you're doing, but baby steps still count as long as you're moving forward and are faithful to it.

Here's a challenge that I think people have. Some people will come in, and they don't respect what they have their hands on. Real estate investing...make no mistake about it...for that last hundred years, real estate investing has created more millionaires, point blank. No one will argue with the fact that it's created more millionaires than any other sort of way to make money online.

But, what will happen is that they'll get involved in real estate, and they'll treat it like a hobby. Well, let me ask you, Mark, do hobbies *make* you money or do they *cost* you money?

Any hobby that I've ever been in has, for sure, cost me money...and anybody I know, it definitely cost them money to have a hobby.

Yeah. People will come in and treat this like a hobby, and they don't respect it as a multi-million dollar business. I know that, before this interview, you and I were talking about a deal that you're working on right now that is what we call a "monster deal". There are deals we've done that produce more for us than some people make in a year, and that's just *one* deal.

Coming where I come from, the deal that we're putting together is more than most of my family makes in four years...and that's the truth.

I'm sitting in the Poconos right now. TC doesn't think I should be here, but it's an awesome opportunity to get away from the hustle and bustle, and for me to sit down and really focus and work on my business instead of in it.

But, at the same time, as we're doing this and putting all these pieces together, this deal comes about. There are many other ones in the pipeline too, but it's just this one that I'm focusing on. The point is, don't try to do ten of them at the same time. Do one...put it together, and move on. This deal stands to make someone over $100,000 in real profit, real money.

It's amazing. Here's a point I want to make in reference to this – about the "hobby mentality" that some people have. One of our students is a guy named Chad who got started with us. We have an email strategy, Mark, where it doesn't cost you anything to email people...there are just a ton of sites out here.

So, we've got him doing what we call the "million dollar email strategy", and he went after it with gusto. Five weeks into it, he still hadn't done his first deal. The sixth week comes into play, and one of the first emails that he put out turned into his first deal, six weeks later.

See, my mentality and my mindset is that

85

I really don't give a rat's behind if it's the first call or the fiftieth call. I don't care if it's the first email or the hundredth email that gets me the deal. Now, understand what I told you earlier about "the better you get, the easier this gets". I am not working with a huge volume of students now. We're very selective with who we will work with. So, the better you get at this, the easier this process gets for you and the less "work" you will have to do and take on.

The deals just start flowing because you start to have that presence where...you know when someone walks into a room, you just know they have that power? You immediately know they're "someone" or that something is going on with them. It just radiates off of us, and it's like you said, we only deal with people that are ready to go.

Mark, it's not *what* you say – and here's another thing for people to write down - it's the *how* you say it that people are listening to. Do you really mean business or is this all just a game to you?

Mark, I come behind you because I believe that with every fiber in my heart. I believe that you can take somebody, a broke person, and you can put them in a brand new suit and spiff them up and send them out into the street. That person that's broke, even though they've got a suit on, even though they've got on a tie and nice shoes, and they're spiffed up and cleaned up, they are *not* going to be treated with respect.

Yet, you can take somebody that is wealthy and put them in a pair of sweats...no matter

86

where you put them out into the marketplace, that man or that woman is *going* to be treated with respect.

Why is that? It's just something that emanates from their being. It's who you are. So, it's not *what* you say that people listen to in our world today, it's *how* you say it that people are really paying attention to.

A lot of people come to us and they're like, "Well, I don't know what to say. What do I say? If they ask me this question, I don't know the answer." Then, just tell them that you don't know the answer.

I've done that before, and when I do that, I feel like, well, I know that I get a step above because everybody else is out there saying "fake it 'til you make it". You don't have to fake it, just be upfront with them…that's what they want.

Well, Mark, what you're really talking about here is one of my favorite topics, and it's called "non-attachment". The easiest way for me to explain this is that I am not attached to any deal, anywhere, at anytime.

Now, Mark, I know you're working on this $100,000 "monster deal", and I know you. I know that if the thing starts to go sideways, if the seller wants you to jump through any sort of a hoop, that you'll pull back, and you'll walk away at a moment's notice.

Without a question.

You are not attached to it in one iota because you know that there's always another

87

one around the corner.

Let me just make it clear to the readers. There's a TV show on NBC called Deal or No Deal? I don't watch the show on a regular basis, I've just seen it a couple of times, but what I've seen, Mark, is a perfect analogy for real estate investing.

These people get up there, and they become emotionally attached to a big sum of money, and they make dumb decisions. They make stupid decisions that cost them a lot of money. Why? Because they become emotionally attached to a big dollar sign that is hanging out there like a carrot, and they want that more. They let good judgment fall to the wayside. It's a perfect analogy to real estate investing.

Greed will get you every time.

I am not attached to any one deal. I will not jump through a hoop for any buyer or seller. We will not do that, and they know that. It's just like the dumb questions that sometimes people will ask. Here's a good one... Because we teach how to invest in real estate with no credit checks, occasionally people will ask me about my credit.

"What do you say when they ask about your credit?" I thought about this and when the last time was that somebody asked me about that, and I couldn't remember when the last time was. They just simply don't ask. The one time that I do remember that happening, Mark, somebody asked me about my credit, and I said "Excuse me? I didn't say I was going to check your credit."

I've never had my credit checked, EVER, on

a deal. I've never had anybody ask that because I'm in there helping them. Like I said, these are all questions that are running through your head, and you're not going to know how it's going to happen until you do it.

Mark, I had a student tell me that they were having a problem with the credit thing, and what I said to this student was, "The owners don't have a problem with it. The only one that's got a problem with this is you. And all they're doing is feeding off of what vibe you're giving them. You have the problem with it, and you're carrying that onto the kitchen table with you."

Now I've got news for you. Mark, do you still remember when you put $1 to $10 down on a deal?

I was shaking like a leaf.

The first time. I remember it. I was like, "Does this really work?" I'm sitting at their kitchen table thinking this to myself. Well, we're about to find out, right? And then...they warmly accept it. Then you're like, "Oh boy!"

There you go! Like we were talking about at the top of the interview, I left the place feeling like I'd taken my shirt off, and there was a big "S" on my chest.

Yeah, I remember the first time very clearly because I was talking to my mentor saying, "There is no way this is going to happen." He said, "Either you can or you can't...either way, you're right."

So, I went in there and, actually, I gave the guy a $20, and he gave me $10 back because I

**told him I couldn't do over $10 down. He gave me
a roll of quarters...and that is no joke.**

**When that happened, it was like hitting the
lottery! Everything I'd read, everything I'd heard,
all the seminars I'd gone to, everybody I heard
talk in interviews like this...everything just hit
me. I walked out of the house and it was like...
BOOM...I know what everybody's talking about
now!**

**I didn't know before then because I had
only read about the theory and only saw it through
other people doing it, but now I'd done it myself,
so it was "real".**

There's a tremendous difference between
going through the motions because you've heard
it works and *knowing* that it works. When I left
that house after putting money down on that
house without a credit check...I was never the
same.

You see, what I do now is I shudder at
that two-week period of hell that I went through.
Because the deals just weren't happening for me,
right? And all I could do during those times was
put the blinders on and just simply put one foot in
front of the other and keep going. I knew that it
worked, I knew that it was going to work for me...
I just needed to keep doing the activities that led
to the results. I knew that if I did that, that the
results would come.

**You stayed focused and persistent...we
can't say it enough, how important that is.**

It's interesting...what I didn't tell you in the
second half of that story is that it took me two

weeks to get the first deal, but the very next day two more deals came! It was that quick. All of that energy that I'd put into the first one just propelled me forward, and then they started coming like crazy. I see this happen all the time.

Mark, I would like to bring this up this next idea for the good of everyone reading this interview...everything is about motion. Real estate has an energy to it...it has emotion to it.

When you get started, the hardest thing is like getting behind this big, old, fat elephant and trying to push the thing up the hill. But, once you get that elephant moving, it becomes easier.

It gets easier, but that's really the time to start pushing harder.

The mistake I see new investors make is that they extend all that energy to "get that elephant moving", and then they take a week or two off once it starts getting easier. Then the elephant stops, but you expect him to keep moving. No. You've got to go back and you've got to start pushing all over again to get that motion going again. But, once you get the elephant going then it becomes like...well, like a knife thru hot butter, as they say in Boston.

It's so key. So many great people get to the 1-yard line — they're pushing that fat elephant, as TC would say, up the hill — and they're getting ready to break over to the other side and then... BOOM. For whatever reason, they give up on their dreams or they have this thing inside of them that keeps them from succeeding and making that deal happen. Sometimes it happens because

people get scared of success.

It's a weird feeling that will come over you...I don't care if you're experienced or not or how big of a deal you're doing or not doing. It's just this weird, uncharted territory feeling. But, when you step outside of your comfort zone...TC, you talk a lot about the comfort zone. What's that phrase that you say that is so powerful? Let our readers know so they can write it down.

"Your comfort zone is your failure zone."

People will go through life, and, as long as they're comfortable – you know, "don't mess with me", "don't mess with my family, I'm comfortable" ...they will live beneath what they really can do. Why? *Because* they're comfortable.

When I left Chicago to come to Florida, Mark, no one backed that move. No one in our family backed it. No one in our circle of influence agreed that this was what we should do. We didn't know anyone down here, and coming to a state that we'd never lived in before...we had no friends here in this area.

Illinois was my comfort zone. I knew, though, that my destiny was in a different zone, and that I had to get out of my comfort zone if I was ever going to make it.

That is so huge. Like I said before, no one knows what goes on behind closed doors in your life to bring you to where you are now until we talk about this kind of stuff.

It's easy to sit on the couch watching a rich guy doing an infomercial and think that you could never have what he has...I'll bet he started out

just like you did, with some kind of struggle that made him get out of his comfort zone and just do it.

You're so right. Now, what I didn't tell you at the top of the interview is that we sold our place up in Illinois to people who wanted a fast closing – within 45 days. So, I had to find our dream house in Florida within 45 days. And it wasn't just any type of house that we wanted. We wanted the "dream house", and I had to get it without a credit check.

Does this sound familiar to anyone reading this? Does this sound, in any way, remotely familiar to when, at the top of the interview, I talked about when I didn't have a choice? I can't tell you, Mark, how many people that "loved us" told us it would never work, the "professionals" told me I'd never find that type of house...

It's so hard because a lot of times, the people that will be the most against you – or negative with you – are the ones that you love the most.

Unfortunately, that is true. And I was very specific on what I wanted in this house. People told me, "That house doesn't exist. Well, it may exist, but you're not going to get it without a credit check." To which I said, "Just watch me."

See, I'm the type of guy that, Mark, you tell me I can't do it, I'm going to do it twice. The first time I'll do it to prove to you that I could do it, and the second time it's "in your face", just in case you weren't paying attention the first time.

So, again, because I didn't have a choice in the matter, we came down here and found what

93

we were looking for, and that one deal changed our lives forever.

Believe you, me, I've been in some uncomfortable places in my life, but it's always propelled me to another level. We're always looking to take our business to another level. We're always pushing and prodding each other to go to another level because we realize that we never want to get "fat and sassy" with what we're doing.

What TC's talking about...that's why I feel so connected and so glad to be around him is that this is the guy who led me through the water. He was standing there, waist-deep, beside me, and he brought me up in front of a group to talk about that kind of stuff.

If anybody knows me, and a lot of people reading this do know me...I'm not *that* **person. I do my thing. I'm quiet. I take care of whatever I need to do, and I'm good with it.**

But, when TC did that, it definitely opened my eyes to a whole new world of so many different things. Him doing that was so powerful, and that's why I'm still, to this day, so glad that that happened.

You about puked your guts out.

I was eating dry toast before I got up there ...and I was only up there a half an hour! And it's not even a big deal because I know what I'm talking about. I know what I'm doing but that's just not "in" some people to do.

When he set me outside of that comfort zone, I knew, deep down inside, that I needed to

do it. And, when I did it, different things started shifting, and the other side of my real estate business started growing without effort. It was always there, but things just started changing and started running smoother and easier, and it was just like, "Wow...what just happened?" All these pieces that he's talking about are so powerful, and it's about taking them one by one.

Its like that movie I told you about where it'll all just come to you when you take charge like that.

Right. TC recommend a movie called *The Secret*. In it, there is something that Jack Canfield said, the guy who wrote *Chicken Soup for the Soul*. He said, "We all know where we want to go." And then he said, "This is like going from New York to California in the fog, and you can only see 200 feet in front of you in the dark, but you just let the road take you where it's going...to take you those 200 feet."

These are the baby steps TC was talking about. You don't have to go out and do huge deals and make $100,000 a deal. Do a $1,000 deal just to build your confidence up. Every deal is going to build your confidence up, right, TC?

Without question. One of the things I want people to know is that is sometimes people will go and they'll hip-hop around like a little bunny rabbit. They'll go from deal to deal, from course to course. I'm a firm believer in that the "magic" is not in a real estate course, it's not in the business opportunity...the "magic" is in you.

People tend to...well let me put it to you

95

this way: what you're seeking to become, you already are...you just need to step into it. People have this thing about talent being a deciding factor. "Well, TC, if I could talk the way that you talk, then I would be talented" or "Mark, if I had your upbringing then I could be successful."

Let me clue you in for a second. I come from a blue-collar background. Second of all, I could not talk until I was five years old. I had a major speech impediment that caused me to not be able to talk. I was made fun of in grade school. I got tough and got into a lot of fights because of it. I've never been the guy that's been the most talented guy out there on the block.

I've talked many times about the fact that I come from a small town and never had money growing up.

You just never know what's in a man or a woman's heart. I can tell you that, doing this for some time now, I can look on the highway, Mark, and it's filled with the carcasses of people way more talented and way more educated than I ever hoped or dreamed of being. So, talent isn't the deciding factor.

It sure is not. I'm not advocating this by any means, but I barely graduated high school. I still, to this day, don't know how I did it, but I graduated with a 1.8. That's the lowest GPA you can graduate with. School is not for everybody. Deena and I travel all over all the time just because that's what we enjoy doing.

I sit beside great people on planes, and I'm talking about real estate. These guys are doctors,

engineers, lawyers...people that are way smarter, intellectually, but yet at the same time they say, "What do I do? I don't want to do this." But, they're traveling all the time, and they don't get to spend time with their children.

It really is sad, and they don't even realize it, most of the time.

One thing I did have as a kid, and that I was very fortunate to have, is that my parents spent a lot of time with us kids. I played a lot of sports when I was a kid, and they were able to show up and be there and watch me. I remember so many kids that didn't have that.

I was the locker room talk. "My mom and dad aren't going to make it."' Like I said, I do not come from a wealthy family, by all means, but the love and everything that comes behind that is powerful, and it showed me that I want to be able to do both. I want to have the money and the love to be able to go to my kid's school functions and church functions. I never get that out of my head. Everyday I think about that because it was so powerful for me.

Mark, some people that are reading this have never been acknowledged before, and I want to say this too because there's people reading this and thinking, "You know what? These guys didn't talk a lick about real estate." Yet, there will be others that feel this interview has been a defining moment in their life in some way.

I have news for you. We can give you all the real estate and "technical" knowledge – the know-how of how to dot the i's and cross the t's.

But, if you have that, and you don't have what we're talking about here and now, then you're going to miss the boat. You'll be off by the side of the road this time next week. You'll be watching reruns of Barnaby Jones, and talking about how this stuff doesn't work. You've got to "get" what we're talking about tonight...this is your foundation. You can get everything else right but get this wrong, and you're not going to make it. You've just got to get your mindset right in order to succeed.

I've talked about this. We're not in the real estate business. Real estate is our product. We are in the marketing business. You have to be persistent with marketing.

So many people talk about having a number one, best-seller novel, but if no one knows about it, it's not going to be a number one, best-seller, that's for sure.

What you have to do is let people know what you're doing. Don't walk around with your head down. Don't be intimidated or afraid to pass your cards around. If you have cards you *should* pass them around. People want what you have, and it's your <u>duty</u> to let them know this even exists.

I still, to this day, TC, I can't believe how many people don't understand what we do because it's so readily available. It's such a great lifestyle once you understand it.

One thing I want to come behind you on this number one, best-seller comment that you made. I'll tell you this – you'll never have a number one, best-seller if you never get out the pen and paper and write it. There are people that are best-selling authors reading this interview *right now*. You have a story, you have a gift, and you haven't done anything with it. Why? Because you're in your comfort zone.

It applies to anything in life, but I would rather Mark tell his story than tell my story any day of the week. I would rather talk about your business than about my business. But I do have a story too, and I do know what it's like to look for quarters in the seat cushions of my sofa to get my family a gallon of milk and a loaf of bread.

So, I hold that up to you all as a banner to let you know that what you're seeking to become you already are...you just need to step into it. You need to let go of the dock. Let go of your comfort zone, and readily and boldly and courageously step into what you know.

It's so powerful to look back and be able to see all this so clearly now...it's why I'm so passionate about helping others reach their goals.

Mark, this has been a long journey as far as trying to find information so that I could reach *my* goals. You see, a course like yours was not available to me when I started out. A course like the one that Vickie and I offer, the materials and the products that we offer...that was not available to me.

My biggest challenge was what to say to a homeowner. Do you tell them that you're an investor or do you not tell them? How do you set this up? What's the psychology of a deal? I would buy these courses, and, to be quite honest, I would fast-forward or turn the pages, and all it

99

would say was, "Talk to the owner." I thought, "You've got to be kidding me!"

Right now, the Internet really has opened things up. There are people besides you and I, Mark, that have some really good stuff out there. The Internet has really opened people up to a whole new world so that you can actually get our material – both ours and Mark's – so that you don't have to make the mistakes that I made.

With the Internet, everything is at our fingertips. We can get online to do research any time of the day or night. It's all right there for you for whenever it fits into your schedule. The greatest thing about this is that, once you understand it, the lifestyle that it brings is awesome.

TC, you know I'm always running around doing stuff. I was in Miami for five months and now I'm in the Poconos – I'm traveling for the next two years. But, I'm still consistently running my business, and that's key. You're either consistent or non-existent. So, I make sure that we're consistently doing at least a deal or two each week.

Mark, you have a clear vision of your life, and of what's possible to do with your life. A friend of mine made a comment to me recently. I hadn't seen him in a couple of years, and he goes, "I just can't see myself as a successful business owner." He's working for some type of corporation right now. He said, "I just can't see myself being a businessman, much less a successful one."

So, how will he ever get past that? No one is going to see what you see. One of the reasons we started a multi-million dollar company the first

100

time, before we lost it to our partner, is that we believed we could, and we believed that we could do it quickly. I just got off the couch, and I did something with it.

You, Mark, believe that you can live the life of your dreams, and so you're doing it. Some of you are saying, "Well, I could never do that." Well, then you're right. I'll align my faith with yours tonight, and I'll agree with you that you can't do it. How does that make you feel?

TC, I can't believe you're being so nice tonight. Personally, I would say bologna because I know where I came from, and I know my background. I know where I started from, and if I can do it, anybody can. If you can read, write and think, you can do it! Wouldn't you agree?

Yeah. I have a saying, "If I could teach a monkey how to dial a telephone, that monkey could take down a deal without a credit check and only $1 to $10 down."

Everyone, this really IS us. Us talking right now is no different than the conversations we have that are one on one. We're here to shine the light, and we understand that the light is brighter the closer you get to the end of the tunnel.

We're so un-scripted...we're just us. I'm not well-polished anyway, but I know that the information inside of us, with application, can take you to levels that you've only dreamed of. But, you've got to dream it and believe it. If you can think it, it will happen. Just really put yourself into that moment.

I remember driving a car and just sitting

101

there with my hand on the wheel, looking out the left side of the window and acting as if I was driving my dream car. Within three months, I had my dream car that I had wanted at that time. I put myself in those shoes. I felt the wind, and I put all five senses toward what was happening to make it come true. When that happens, you're creating your own déjà vu, in essence. Wouldn't you agree, TC?

Without question.

I get goose bumps talking about it because it's so amazing. People will walk around saying, "How do you guys so it?!" I'm thinking, "We just do it...that's how we do it." Really, there's no secret.

Well, Mark, I think it comes back to what you said you felt passion about tonight for this interview...about sharing how it all starts with the first deal. Had you not had the guts and tenacity to get out of your comfort zone and get your first deal done, where would you be right now?

I don't even want to talk about that.

Your whole life changes with the first deal, so if I could encourage you tonight to do one thing, it would be to get your first deal done. Now, Mark, I believe you said you had a gentleman email you today from California saying that he's just taking down deals left and right in California – that's his reality. And, yet, you've got other people that live there and say, "Oh, you can't do that."

Yeah. "You can't take down deals in a hot market that's appreciating at 32% to 34% per year. Come on, TC."

Yet, here's a guy casually writing in to you saying that he's just taking down deal after deal in one of the hottest markets in the country. My hat's off to a guy like that.

You said something a couple weeks back, Mark, that I've just held onto...and that is that we define our markets. People ask me all the time, "Well, what about this market we're in?" and my response is, "We define the market."

If you have the specialized knowledge and you take action, you can define your market too. The only difference between me and you is I have specialized knowledge, and I get out of my own way. The only difference between Mark and you is that Mark has specialized knowledge, and he takes action...that's it. If you have the specialized knowledge, and you pay the same price that we have paid, along the way, then you can have what we have.

The "price" he's talking about paying is working hard and working towards your goals. It has nothing to do with money...it has to do with everything. Wouldn't you agree, TC?

Well, I don't agree completely with that. In some cases, it *is* a financial price. In other cases, it isn't. For some of you reading this, you've already got the information, you've already got the education, you've already paid that price. You've already struggled through having a full-time job and still coming home and getting your butt in

103

that little home office of yours to start working the business at night and on the weekends.

Those that pay the price and get in there and will do what they know they need to do, instead of sitting on the couch and turning on the TV, *that's* a price. Like you said, Mark, that's not a financial price, but it's still a heavy price to pay. I call it the "high road verses low road" mentality.

So, we've got six months left in this year. In another couple of months they're going to put the Christmas trees out. It seems like they're putting that stuff out earlier and earlier as I get older. Between now and Christmas, there will be people that can have life-transforming experiences that are reading this, and they're going to have the best Christmas of their life. Do you want to know who that person is? It's going to be the person that takes the high road more than they take the low road every single day.

What's the high road versus the low road to you, TC?

The high road is getting home from work, getting your dinner eaten and then, instead of lying on the couch, it's going to your home office and getting to work, working your real estate business...that is the high road.

And here's the low road: you get home from work, and you're tired...it's a Monday, and you hate Mondays, and you say. "You know what, I'm kind of tired anyhow, and I sort of got to bed late last night, and my favorite show is on tonight, so I'm going to get some sleep and I'll hit this hard tomorrow." And then Tuesday comes and you say, "You know what, another day and

104

I'll really be rested up" and the rest of the week turns out pretty much the same way.

The low road is just as simple as taking the high road. Those of you that take the high road do what you know you need to do. You do what you know will get you results and put the money in your bank account. Those that take the high road more times than they take the low road will have a Christmas this year like they never dreamed of!

Absolutely. Not only that, but I think the high road is easier. It's easier because you're not down on yourself, you're not falling down and digging yourself deeper and deeper into a hole you can't climb out of.

The hard way *is* the easy way. What we teach is very, very simple. I want to make this distinction for a minute. What we teach is very *simple*, but it's not *easy*. It's not easy because it requires effort, it requires commitment, it requires you to get out of your comfort zone. But, it *is* simple once you do it and see for yourself. Deals aren't going to knock on your door and say, "Here I am...take me down." But, if you'll get out of your comfort zone, it's a very simple business.

What I can tell you, though, is that those deals come easier with the Internet...and easier every day as it gets better. Wouldn't you agree with that? It's direct-mail at it's best. You only talk to people that want to talk to you about what you're offering. You're not mass-marketing...you don't have to.

Well, Mark, the Internet gives us, the investor, an unfair advantage. There's a tidal wave of opportunity that is sweeping our country. I have news for you. Twenty years from now our grandkids are going to look at us and go, "You guys were alive during that period of time? You had this sort of an opportunity and you did nothing with it? Oh, I would give anything to just be alive during that time." That's the time we live in right now.

And then my question to them would be, "Would you really?" We're all in that opportunity right now. It's just in its infant stages, in my eyes. It's growing by leaps and bounds daily.

Yeah, and I think that, for whatever reason, there are people reading this that never read books like this, and it might even be their first time and they think they're doing it by accident. But, I just don't think that they are. I think that this is your wake-up call. What you do with it...where there's inspiration there's obligation. You've been inspired tonight. We've given you everything we could give to you. Now it's going to be your call to make.

You can take down deals anywhere. I don't care if you're in California or wherever. You can take down deals in Wisconsin, Florida...it doesn't matter what market, slow, fast, or anything because that doesn't matter. That's all excuses.
You create your own market, especially when you have the tools that TC talks about and teaches. What he and Vickie have done is just simply amazing. And, like you said, you didn't

106

even intend for all that to happen right, TC?

Yeah. I wasn't in my jacuzzi one night, and the clouds parted, and I got divine inspiration and said, "Hey I'm going to be a guru" or "I'm going to sell real estate information."

But you said something earlier...it's like sometimes people say, "Well, if you're so successful in real estate than why are you marketing information?" Duh...why would I not? It's an income stream, and who said you can't do both?

First of all, we didn't start out this way, but we've reached a point where we sort of live vicariously though our students. It's like throwing a rope back. I know what the frustration is like, and I know some of the roadblocks that I encountered, and I know what was out there when I was doing this and desperately, desperately trying to get started and not getting the information and the technology that I needed to make things happen. I know what that's like, and, at some point, you've got to throw a rope back and you've got to help other people out.

Not only that, but just having that information...like you said, it was never in my realm of being an information person, but, at the same time, we've been there. We're real people just like you...no different, except that we took... what would you call it? What road, TC?

That would be the high road.

The "high road". And we stepped outside of our comfort zones. You could ask TC about that...

107

I stepped *way* outside of mine. I was perfectly comfortable where I was at.

I guess we haven't talked about this, but when we talk about the investing we still do, we're not talking about cracked-out houses where you've got to go with a bulletproof vest on because, trust me, I've been there, and I don't recommend it. I know that some of you reading this know exactly what I'm talking about. I've been there. I've had cops run after me and tackle me thinking that I'm the suspect.

We're not talking about houses like that. I'm also not talking about going out and buying a house, fixing it up, and making $3,000 on it after you spent eight months rehabbing it.

We're talking nice homes, dream homes. TC bought his dream home like this. The house TC is talking about is a $640,000 house that he got with zero credit checks. The guy didn't even think about it. He actually told him, "Please, just take it." $640,000 home with zero credit check and zero cash out of his own pocket. Believe me when I tell you, those deals are available all day long.

Mark, first of all, I make no apologies for marketing real estate information...cutting-edge information, actually. I'm not so self-righteous as to say that other products and information are not good.

I don't talk about, nor does Mark talk about what he "thinks" will work. We talk about what we *know*, beyond any shadow of a doubt, will work. It is not bias. Opportunity is not bias. It *will* work for you no matter who you are, if you're willing to take the time to work the system.

It's like a recipe. You give a broke person a recipe to bake a cake, and if you give a rich or talented person the same recipe, they'll both bake the same cakes. You're not going to get a different result. That's what we're talking about. There's a major difference between talking theory and talking cutting-edge...what you know works, day in day out. That, to me, is the bottom line.

We've covered a lot of stuff here, TC . . . do you think it's all getting through?

I think that there is a law, Mark, that peoples' brains automatically shut off after 45 minutes of sitting.

Well, then you need to get up and walk around, like TC and I do. TC is pacing right now for sure, and I'm pacing all over the place. It's because this stuff is so powerful and so overwhelming. Once you guys understand that... isn't that so funny that successful people learn more every day? I can't even remember the last time I watched TV, as opposed to a movie that is educating me on something I want to know about.

Mark you need to watch Deal or No Deal.

I've seen it...at two o'clock in the morning when I can't sleep. But there are so many neat things that come with that — with the constant learning.
I've been the person who got this book and is diving into it and is now sitting there going, "Ok what do I do now? How do I do this?" Stop

thinking about all that. Just concentrate on one thing, one deal. Let it come to you. Put it into motion. Get it going. You don't have to get it right, just get it going. It doesn't have to be perfect, that's for sure...just do it. The Nike slogan still prevails "Just do it." Maybe you're not going to be the best in the beginning, but you're going to be in motion...and not just motion but *forward* motion.

Well, I would come behind you, Mark, and I would say "just do it" until you get the first deal. Commit to doing it until you get the first deal. Then, if you want to quit and take your bat and ball and go find somewhere else to play, you can do that, but at least do it on your terms, not on somebody else's.

And I've never know anybody to quit once they've done their first deal. I've known people that have lost money and don't quit. It's not about that. They just know that the opportunity lies in front of them.

Just jump in a plane — it amazes me everyday. If we can jump in a plane and fly so many thousands of feet in the air and just look down. Look down at this opportunity that's around us. There's enough for all of us...and then some.

Without question, your time is now...there's no tomorrow. I've been the guy that says, "I'm going to go on a diet next Thursday, when it's my birthday, and I'm going to be excited." No. If you're ready to do it, you're ready to do it.

You know who you are. You're sitting at the edge of your seat and you're like, "It's my time." So, TC, do you want to talk about the offer?

Let me just come behind you and tell you what I hear all the time...it's, "'Someday, I'm going to do this. Someday I'm going to get going." I actually had a prospective student contact me a year ago, in January, and say, "You know what, I've got some things going on in my life right now that I'm going to get all cleared out in the next thirty days. When I do, I'm gonna come after it, and I'm going to be your biggest success story."

You know Mark, for thirty days I don't hear from that prospective student. But, you know what? Honestly, what happened a year later, in January, is that I got the same email...nothing had changed in that person's life.

If you think that something's going to change for you thirty days from now, I have some bad news for you. Thirty days from now you're going to have a fresh, whole new slew of challenges that you don't even know about today.

So, for those that talk about, "Someday, I'm going to do this..." The best diets always happen "someday" from now. "One day I'm going to do this..." "Someday..." and "One day..." are not on my calendar.

Mine either...there's no need for it and no time...we only have one life to live, so I take action now.

Mark, I have a couple of things to say as my closing remarks, if you don't mind. Accountability is absolute, and I know that there are people reading this and wondering if what we said here is going to change their lives because they're sick and tired of being sick and tired.

To Receive Your $247 In Free Bonuses: www.TheInsiderSecretsGifts.com

Well, we've given you a huge jumpstart here tonight. So, what I want you to do is just one thing, and that's honor your word. If you say you're going to do it, then do it.

Some of you don't have your spouses behind you because all you've done so far is talked a good talk...you haven't walked your walk yet. So, you need to step up to the plate and start walking the walk...period.

If you say you're going to do it then, by God, you do it. But, if you're not...if you have no intentions of doing it, then don't even speak about it. There's too much "talk" going on nowadays. People talk a good talk, but they don't walk their walk.

If you're going to make a decision to change your life, then get your hand raised up in the air and honor your personal decision to do that. Commit yourself to doing that first deal, no matter what, and we'll stand with you.

Mark, thank you so much for inviting me to talk with you tonight. I really appreciate it.

Absolutely. TC, thank you very much for taking time out of your night and for getting on board with me to tell everybody to just go out there and do it. You owe it to yourself and everybody around you that you love. It's fun, so enjoy it and have fun doing it. So, again, thank you.

Thank you Mark.

Have a great night.

"Be careful the environment you choose for it will shape you; be careful the friends you choose for you will become like them."

- W. Clement Stone

"I have not failed 700 times. I have not failed once. I have succeeded in proving that those 700 ways will not work. When I have eliminated the ways that will not work, I will find the way that will work."

- Thomas Edison; Inventor

"Most of the important things in the world have been accomplished by people who have kept on trying when there seemed to be no hope at all."
- Dale Carnegie; Author

"I do not think that there is any other quality so essential to success of any kind as the quality of perseverance. It overcomes almost everything, even nature."
- John D. Rockefeller;
Standard Oil Co. Co-Founder

Chapter Four
Interview with Doug Doebler

Today we've got Doug Doebler taking time out of his busy day to talk with us. We call him the "hundred million dollar condo guy".

What we are going to do is keep with that theme and shine the light and expose you to why doing the first deal is so important and will propel you from selling peanut brittle to selling hundreds of millions of dollars in pre-construction condos.

Yes that's the story, Mark, you got it.

Doug, how about you give us a quick background of where you started from, where you are now, and what you're working on now?

Sure, Mark. I am from rural, upstate New York near Rochester. That real estate market has stayed pretty neutral for about 22 years...at least as long as I've been in the business. It's not been like a California or the East Coast or the Florida market.

My family is in the residential real estate business. My father had a local residential real estate company, so I grew up in the business.

I think I was born an entrepreneur. As you just mentioned, when I started out as a young guy, I would sell flowers in front of my father's office, and I also sold peanut brittle when I was a cub scout (I won a watch for my efforts).

There was a little warehouse behind my

115

father's real estate office. I used to buy bicycles, fix them up and sell them, and then I graduated to cars. I had access to estate sales. They were selling houses, and, once in a while, there would be a car for sale, so I would buy the car for about $500. Then, I would fix it up and sell it for a couple grand. This was all at 15 and 16 years old. Then, I graduated to what we want to talk about today...real estate.

Sounds like you were born to be a salesman.

My first deal was a $29,900 house that I bought the year I went to college. Actually, I'd gone to college to be a car dealer...I spent half of my time in college studying the automotive business. Anyway, my first house I bought with a student loan. I'm talking 25-26 years ago (I'm in my mid-40's now).

It was a VA assumable mortgage I think I put down $2,000 or $3,000 and assumed the mortgage. I took the house, cleaned it up a little bit and rented it for a couple of years. Then I sold it, and made a little profit, so I bought another house.

It just kind of went on from there. I bought houses that were $10,000 to $15,000 that were real wrecks and fixed them up. I never did a lot of heavy repair or maintenance myself. I would hire that out to be done, or just tidy them up some. I never did a total rebuild or anything.

Doug, you said you were born an entrepreneur. I believe we all have the entrepreneurial spirit instilled in us, it's just what

116

we do with it because sometimes we get out of focus. So, just because you're an entrepreneur doesn't always mean that it's easy to make money right?

No, not at all. You can be a scattered entrepreneur. I have friends who, every week they have some new crazy idea, and they're all chasing a million bucks every week, but they never do anything because they just aren't focused enough.

They go from one thing to another to another. The key is to get more focused. Decide what you want to do and go for it. Hey, if it doesn't work out, then move on to the next thing. But, at least give it a full run for it.

Exactly. Don't you think that, a lot of times, people think that success is just huge glitz and glamour?

Yet, it's the daily actions – or lack of taking action – of people that keeps them from being the greatest they can be. Without action, they'll just stay miserable and not know how they can pay the bills. Successful people take action...and it's not always glamorous, but they see that they need to do it and then they go out there and do it.

Success is really just planting your feet on the ground and focusing on one or two different ways to become an expert at what you do. Then, if you want to divert from there, then do that.

But it's not like Doug was selling houses, then next week he's selling vitamins, then next week he was doing something else. He stayed with the same thing...kept in the groove...and

just continued to grind it out every day.

Yes, what I think I was doing was building my entrepreneurial muscle by moving from selling peanut brittle as a cub scout to being a real estate entrepreneur that sells hundreds of millions in condos. It was a whole series of processes throughout the early years.

I started out with those couple of single family homes, and then I graduated to co-buying them and selling them for a $10,000 to $15,000 profit. Then I graduated to doing some multi-family homes that I kept for many years and rented out – they had a good cash flow and I was able to pay off the mortgage.

I still have 2 of those houses that I've had for over 15 years. The mortgages are now paid off, and it feels pretty good when the rent checks come in, knowing I can finally put that money in my pocket instead of using it to pay the mortgage payment as I did for the 15 years. That was a 15-year process, so, yes, growth has taken time, but I have consistently worked to build that up over the years.

Doug, let's go back to your first deal...when you were right around 18 years old.

What were you thinking as you started putting that together? Are you thinking, "God, I'm going to fail, I'm going to loose everything?"

A lot of people focus their energy on what *could* happen as opposed to all the good stuff that can happen. Put yourself back in the shoes of our readers when they're out there making those first deals...were you scared to death at first or were you excited?

118

I think I was both. I was excited because here I was, an 18-year-old kid, buying a house. Maybe I had the benefit of my family being in the real estate business, but my father did not buy and sell houses, so that wasn't part of my upbringing. I kind of understood real estate, and I had my real estate license at that time. Actually, now that I think about it, I got a commission on selling that house to myself, and that helped pay for my down payment. It was a creative transaction – a student loan and some commission.

I mean, I didn't have any money. I was 18 years old and taking on the responsibility of running the ads and getting it rented. I was in college, so my mother collected the rent for me and paid the mortgage payment for me. I think she had to do an eviction once for me too, when I was away at college. I came back from college in the summer and sold the place and made a few bucks and went on to buy the next house.

So, when people say they don't have time to do it, it's bologna, right?

Oh, yeah. I'm sure I was nervous and scared, but I was also excited because I was moving on. I had been buying and selling cars for 3 years, and this was the next thing.

The houses I bought started out as single family and then progressed to multi-family. Then, I bought some land and farmland and larger 100+ acre land tracts.

Then, I started developing the land, in some cases. Just buying it and splitting it off into 5 acre lots. I got hooked up with a builder, and we

119

started building some houses on the land. I sold the houses and the land, so that was kind of my next progression in the business.

I then bought some land and had to have a road built and town water lines installed, as well as all of the utilities...it was like a sub-division. I had to meet all of the approvals of the town, and all that. That was an interesting and difficult process, but once again I was flexing my entrepreneurial muscles.

Flexing it? Sounds like you were becoming The Hulk (laughing)!

It was fun. Then, I graduated into investing in Florida pre-construction condos. These were condos ranging in price between $250,000 to over $1 million dollars. Then, I got to watch how that business operated. After that, I got my broker's license in Florida, and was then brokering those condos, which is what I am currently doing.

So, Doug, people might be thinking that you have had it easy this whole time, and that you were just probably playing around. Can you shine the light on the 25-some years that it took you to do all that?

What kind of houses prices you were at in the beginning? I know you kind of touched on it already, but just explain where you started. I mean, you didn't just start right out of the gate brokering hundreds of millions of dollars in condos overnight, right? This was a long process that actually came about from the pain of losing your 20-year relationship with the builder, right?

Yes, it was a 25+-year process. I came from a middle class conservative family. I didn't have loads of money behind me to do these things. I remember getting my loans from the local banker back in the days when they pretty much shook your hand and gave you a chance at giving you a loan.

I had to do the same things that everybody else has to do too – I had mortgages on houses. When I bought the farmland, the farmers would actually carry the mortgage for me...I used creative financing.

Back when it probably didn't even have a name and had never been called that.

Probably the longest "job" I had was when I was selling new construction homes for a builder. These houses ranged in price from $80,000 to $300,000. My average sale price ranged from $160,000.00 to $170,000 for many years. I sat in the model home pretty much six days a week, and pretty much worked every weekend. I worked all the time – 70 to 75 hours per week. I paid my dues, sold a lot of new homes, and learned a lot about customer follow up and customer service.

I was pretty successful. Then I took on about 3 or 4 salespeople for this builder, and helped him grow his sales from 20-30 per year up to about 70 units per year.

All of a sudden, two years ago, the builder decided I was making too much money, so they wanted to take the salespeople in-house and gave me the option to work in-house at a substantially reduced income. Obviously, I didn't want to do that, and I was kind of upset because I had spent

121

10 to 15 years of my life building this up for the company, and they were basically shutting me down or taking my sales operation over, so I got mad and quit. Then, I looked for something new to do, and that is when I came across the Florida pre-construction condo business.

Well, you have touched upon a lot of things that people need to know. Sometimes change isn't easy — it takes time, and some people are just not willing to wait.

I know you said one time that you jumped in your truck, and it was 10 to 13 degrees below zero in Rochester NY. You were heading to an open house knowing that no one was going to show up with that kind of temperature...can you tell us a little more?

I think your buddy said you were going through a mid-life crisis, but it turned out to be the best mid-life crisis, right?

Oh, yes. I think that what happened to me was the best thing that could have happened because I moved on to the next thing, which has led to substantially better things that I probably would not have done if that hadn't happened.

I was stuck in the "rat race" that I had been in for 20 years. I mean, I was successful. I was doing ok — I had a nice house and a nice car. But you're right...there was more to be done. I'm living in a house in Up State New York now, and I am looking out my window overlooking my driveway...that is right where I was sitting when I you told that story.

Yes, I remember.

I was driving out of my driveway here on my way to the open house on a Saturday morning ...it was about 11 o'clock. The thermometer in my Jeep Cherokee said minus 11 degrees, and I said to myself, "Who in the heck is going to come to an open house in this kind of weather," but I had to go sit there. The next day, Sunday, it was minus 13 degrees, and I had to go do it again.

I started to think that I really need to do something different. I wasn't really happy with what I was doing, but I stuck with it anyway. I did some consulting work, took some classes in mentoring, and then I met Frank McKinney. I remember saying to him, "Man, Frank, I hate doing these open houses. I go there 70 hours per week and sit. Sometimes people come, and sometimes they don't."

He looked at me square in the eye and said, "If you're doing something that you say you hate, then why are doing it? You have to do something that you are passionate about. If you're not passionate about it, then you're not going to be successful at it, so you need to find something else to do."

Well, that kind of hit me square in the eyes, and that's when I realized that I really needed to just go and do something else.

So, when the builder came to you and proposed that you take a pay cut, that was like a blessing in disguise, wouldn't you say, Doug?

Yes, now I would. I was really mad. I mean really, really angry, and it was tough. But, luckily for me, I had a real estate business-building

123

coach, Rich Levin, that I was working with. Rich was kind of like my psychologist. I would talk to him about all of it, and he really helped me understand what was going on and helped me out. He showed me how to not look at it as my business being destroyed, but to look at it as an opportunity to move on and look for something else.

It's funny because I was at a charity golf tournament for Habitat For Humanity last week, and I sat with this builder and his 2 sons, who I had worked with for those 20 years. I told them about my new success, and they were very happy for me, and jokingly said, "The best thing we ever did was to can your butt!" I was really angry at him for a couple years, but now we can joke about it. They are very happy for me that I'm successful, and I'm very happy that they pulled what they did.

The other thing that I haven't mentioned is that my father was their primary salesperson back in the 70's, so not only was it a twenty-year run for me, but it was also a twenty-year run for my father. So, that was really forty years of my family working in their operation, and one day, for them to say, "You're making to much money and we're going to take this inside," was just crazy.

There are a couple of things you could have done. You could have very easily put your tail between your legs and went out and got another job doing the same old thing that you said you hated anyways, or you could have done exactly what you did.

You said that you were "lucky enough" for all that to have happened. I don't think you were

lucky at all. I think you were just setting yourself up to move on to bigger things, not knowing what would happen in the future or what was going to happen with Rich, your coach. And then you realized that having a coach or mentor was so valuable to you.

I give full credit to Rich Levin, the one mentor I was working with at that time. He was a real estate business building coach. I had also done a program with Frank McKinney – he was the "big picture, think outside the box" kind of guy. He helped me understand that there were huge opportunities out there and were much, much bigger things that I could do. But, I had to build the mindset to do them first. Luckily, I had those gentlemen to help me.

Then I had hired a technician guy who designed my website and kind of created in my mind, the kind of new business that I could create. If it wasn't for him, I wouldn't have gotten such a quick start. In six months, we accomplished what a lot of people would have messed around with for 2 or 3 years.

The only reason I accomplished it in 6 months was because I was paying big bucks in fees to learn how to start my business in the Internet market. And, I was very glad that I did that because it gave me a really big quick start. If I hadn't had that head start, I probably would have stumbled around with it and then given up, so I support the use of mentors and coaches 100%.

Oh absolutely. They have been where you are, and they know where you want to go. A lot

of times they are very detached from you, and from a non-attached approach, you accomplish so much more.

I think we all set limits on ourselves as to how big we can get, or what is even possible, yet a lot of times we don't even know what is available to us. When you unlock that side of you, the sky is the limit.

It's an opportunity to get a jump-start on what you want to do.

So, Doug, in the beginning you said you were happy, scared and excited about getting into the real estate business. Don't you think a lot of people think that we are *just in the real estate business*?

You said something about having a web page. And it's not anything fancy, by all means, right, Doug? People over-think it and think you have to have a really fancy and pricey website to do business.

My webpage is just 1 page. It is really simple. I don't think people believe me when I say that I sold close to $200,000,000 in real estate off that simple website.

It's not a stupid-looking webpage, it's just really simple. It's focused. It's targeted. And it was created by someone who is successful. I'm still using that webpage that I created two years ago because it works.

It's awesome having those systems in place. Not only that, but it's great too because, once you have it up and going, you're done with

it. Wouldn't you say that, Doug?

Yes. We created a good follow-up program... that's imperative to have also. That's what my 20 years of working in the Real Estate Sales Industry has taught me. It's really important to follow up with your customers and to provide the best customer service you can.

A lot of real estate people I bump into just really don't have that type of mentality, and I think that's just wrong. I know that is why I am successful...because I have always provided great customer service.

I just received an email from one of my customers that bought a condo from me about a year and half ago, and they are looking for some photos. Most guys would just ignore them, but I will find them photos of the building they bought in, and I will get them to them by Monday. That way, they will be happy, and they will tell their friends – and that just means more business for me. But, then again, I learned that from the new housing sales that I was in.

That's great Doug. I believe you said it was October of 2004 that you sat down to create "Doug's Ideal Life" and that you were going to go at it full speed ahead.

So, what is your goal? You said you were making a decent living, but it wasn't millions of dollars. Can you tell people how much you are currently making per year and what your goals are to do in the current and future years?

Or maybe you tell them, instead, what your total real estate sales are now and what they're going to be in the future.

127

Then, let's talk about how that is different from what your goals were in January, 2005.

For many years in the home business, $3 million to $5 million in sales equated to about $200,000 in gross commissions, so I ended up with a yearly income of about $120,00 to $130,000. For my upstate New York area, that's really good. I kind of cruised along with that kind of income for a few years.

In October, 2004, you were saying that your goal was to do how many millions of dollars worth of sales and in January, 2005? And this would be with you starting a brand new venture that you weren't really that familiar with, right?

Yes. My goal was to do one deal in the month of January, 2005, but the new home business I was in was done for me. Luckily, with the real estate business, you kind of create a little pipeline of income, so I had 6 to 8 months of income coming from deals that I have sold previously.

So then we created this webpage to sell pre-construction condos in Florida...but I live in New York. The goal was to sell one unit in January, 2005. So, we started marketing it, and we ended up selling about $19 million worth in the month of January – and we did all of that, pretty much, in one weekend.

So, now you're looking at – in about 30 days – I did about 5 years worth of sales like I would have done if I was still in the new house business. That was really exciting, and I got a real charge out of that.

So, in that time frame of 30 days, you did $19 million, right?

Yes, I still remember Frank McKinney and I talked about creating a lifestyle. What Frank had taught me about when you're moving into a new job or a new venture, think about what you want your lifestyle to be first...and then try to create, find or build a job or business around that.

At that time it was wintertime in the middle of New York, and I knew I needed to find something so that I could run back and forth to Florida. I have no children, so I had the flexibility of doing that, and that's why the Florida thing worked so well.

I wanted to work from my house. I live on this beautiful lake in the Finger Lakes region of upstate New York. I wanted to be able to sit out on the patio with my cell phone and wireless laptop computer and do my work Plus, I wanted the flexibility to travel and also to be able to work in my yard or play on the lake when I wanted too. That is what I really wanted to do, and so that's what I did.

I get emails, and I talk to people all the time, and they don't think that some of the stuff that you and I or Frank do is real. They ask, "How in the world do you do that?" But, it all starts with creating that ideal life...thinking about it and putting it on paper. A lot of people will complain about it all day long, but when the rubber hits the road, they need to sit down and create this for themselves.

I know I don't want to be sitting in the cold

in the winter. I want to be able to sit at my house and do whatever I want to do. When you sit down and really make that commitment to yourself, things will start happening, wouldn't you say, Doug?

Oh, yes. You know, I was just sitting here thinking, "Man, I really hate working every single weekend." Then, I built this house on the lake, and I stopped working weekends. So, you don't go look for a new house sales job because what you'll end up doing is working all weekend. You need to find what it is that you can do to have your weekends back to sit out by this beautiful lake and enjoy life.

That's what made me think of this new website. Like we were talking about earlier, first it was doing $19 million in pre-construction condo sales, and now we have moved on to multiple sales in a month and we're doing $10 to $15 million a month. In 2005, we did $100 million in condo pre-construction sales in Florida compared to the two years prior of new home sales volume of $4-$5 million. We will have a similar sales volume in 2006. In January, 2005, we did $20 million in sales, and that was our first, really big success. Then, we moved on to doing that over and over again.

That's what it's all about...make your business duplicate-able.

After that, I was staying at the hotels in South Beach, Florida. I wasn't really working too hard...just sitting at the pool, in my shorts, making phone calls, working on my computer, and selling condos. The condos that we were selling were pre-construction condos, which meant that they weren't built yet, so most of our sales are from talking to people on the phone and trading emails.

They're not built yet, so it's pretty much just interacting with the customer via phone and Internet. We ended up with sales of around $100 million in 2005 as compared to $4 million to $5 million dollar sales in prior years in the Rochester New York area. My total gross commissions went from $200,000 to a couple of million dollars.

Doug, talk about the difference in hours. You were working 70+ hours per week in new home sales and not making a lot of money. What kinds of hours are you putting in now?

I don't work 70–80 hours per week anymore. I have the freedom to work when I want to. I'm sitting on my patio right now. I travel around and work when I want. Sometimes I work 60 hours, and sometimes I only work 20 hours a week.

It's a much "happier" operation then it was before. I don't have to sit at open houses in below-zero weather with a coat and tie on not knowing if anyone is going to show up. Now, I can do what I want and control what I do. So, I'm much happier now.

With all the money aside, Doug, I think that if we do have to work 70 or 80 hours a week, just having the freedom to do what we want, whenever we want, and doing it for ourselves is worth more than millions of dollars.

Absolutely, because you'll be happier, have less stress and a better mentality.

I think it goes hand in hand. It's another piece of the puzzle. As all of that is happening, you start to become more clear, and you begin to see the bigger opportunities right in front of you. Some of them have always been there, it's just that you never knew that before because you were always so busy doing stuff and working hard for someone else.

People come to us and say, "Everything you do turns to gold." Well, that's not really the case. It's just the way *they* see it because that's what they think. They don't see all the hard work that goes into it. We all fail every day. Just like your website...I'm sure you're working at it everyday in some way by tweaking it, making it better, etc.

Opportunities hit me every single day. I had a person call me from Costa Rica wanting me to sell his condos for him. I had another one call me from the Bahamas wanting the same thing. This morning, I had a gentleman call me that has ties with a lot of oil people...that could be a huge opportunity for me.

So, everyday these things are happening. If I had a 9 to 5 job, none of these things would be happening to me. So, I do get to meet a lot of really interesting people. It's really fun. Almost every day or every week there is something new or exciting going on. It's not monotonous like the old program.

Yeah. You're not just showing up and going through the motions. Now you have a meaning in life...a reason to get up and work towards what you want. Just like Frank says, "It doesn't matter if you make a million dollars, as long as you are doing it for you."

Now, I would like to veer off this for a little bit and talk about the power of networking. That's how we met. Never in a million years did I think I would be talking to you right now — that is what is so great about networking. You go to these events and nothing really exciting may happen. But you meet people there and keep the relationships alive by becoming a person of value as you talk to them, see if you help them, you share ideas, etc.

Yes. The people that are doing bigger and better things than you are — those are the people that you want to learn from. Talk to them, communicate, offer them something. At the same time, be available for the people behind you so that you can help them get going as well.

I always try to do that, and I always get that in return from people that I think of as mentors and big players. I think that, if you put yourself in a position to give, you always receive from others.

Absolutely. I think that's so important. When you and I met, we had no idea anything like this was going to happen 16 to 18 months later. We had dreams and goals, and we were determined to make things happen. We have committed to the process, and I think that is another step that people have to make is that

133

step towards commitment.

You also have to continue to network and build your associations with friendship. You really have to put yourself out there with everyone you meet.

That is key in being successful. I go to more seminars and networking events now then I did in the beginning.

There's a seminar in Tampa...you and I have been there 4 times already. But you never know when you might meet someone or get something else out of it, so we keep going back.

Doug, you just said something that is key. You might go to these events, and you might not learn anything. Like at the event where I met you, I didn't learn anything, but meeting and talking with you was worth the trip to Michigan.

Yes. I met you, and I met a customer up there also. The networking with that customer... well, he has given my sales a tremendous boost. And none of this would have ever happened if we didn't go. I mean, you and I just ended up sitting out in the hallway a lot and just chatted.

That is what comes with the power of association — being there, being a part of it, and meeting people. We see this so many times... people show up, but they don't do anything. People just drop off and quit going. But, like you and I, we always seem to be going to the same events, and we keep going over and over

again. **The repetition of going and people seeing you there...then they know that you are really serious. People will start to latch onto you and can start associating you with a being a do-er and understanding who's not doing it. It's all about getting associated with the right people and getting things going, correct?**

Absolutely. Networking is the key...you have to know people. Networking and real estate events are so huge, it is unbelievable. There is so much potential. We know people that have a list of 5,000 people and some have 100,000 people... I know a guy that has a list of a couple million people.

Doug, do you think your business would be where it is now if you were not optimizing or using the Internet?

No way because I sold a substantial amount of real estate in Miami last year, and I don't even live there. I dare say that I was one of the top real estate sales agents in the Miami area in 2005. It's a mystery to the other real estate people there. They wonder how I can do that and not even live there. Well, I use the power of the Internet. I also used the power of Networking. One of my high school buddies introduced me to a large developer in Miami. He had close to 1000 condos to be sold in a 2 year period. We hit it off & I had my developer connection and access to $100's of millions worth of pre-construction condos in Florida and other locations. Now I had the buyer list & the inventory list. I just needed to put them together.

135

If you're not using the Internet today, it's like riding around in a horse and buggy in today's market. Why would anyone think about doing it any other way? So many people trip up about these fancy websites, and they don't need it. Just get something simple, and get it out there.

That's like when I was working with my technician coach, and I wanted everything to be perfect. I kept wanting to make changes, and he looked at me and said, "If this site isn't up and running by Wednesday, don't ever call me back." He said, "Doug, it doesn't have to be an A+ job. It can be a C+. Lets just get it online, and let's see what we can do with it...we can make changes as we go."

So, I put it online, started running ads on Google, and, all of the sudden, my name started coming up all over. It was pretty exciting, and I thought, "What do I do now?" I just made a few changes to it, and it's still, today, about that C+ job that I did back then, but I have gotten over 5,000 prospects off of it, and it does the job.

Now, granted, this doesn't happen overnight ...it was a 2-year process...you get one email at a time. It's a slow process, but it pays off. I always look at it like this: It's just me and one assistant, and I make over $1 million per year. Then, I look at the top real estate agents in the market where I live, and they bring in several hundred thousands a year, but they have a lot of people working for them – they have the big office they pay for, taxes, and everything else. Me? I work out of my home with one assistant. I attribute that to the power of the Internet, and the power of the very optimized follow-up program that I have.

Like you're saying, "I want to get it an A+ level," but it's all bologna when we try to do that because how in the world would we even know what an A+ looks like when we have never even done one? So, the C+ is an A+ to most people because it is up and going. You can always add stuff, delete stuff and move things around. I haven't touched my stuff in over 18 months now.

And, often times, people have to remember that a lot of people who sell products and are successful at it are often the ones that created them at their kitchen table, not products that they went out and spent tens of thousands of dollars on to get produced.

We know a guy that does that, and he makes over $7 million to $10 million per year, but it's not fancy or glamorous...it's just getting valuable information out there, and that is what's important. Getting valuable information out is what people want, so that's what we do. All the webpage is doing is...it's like dating, it's your first wink, right, Doug?

Yes, that's correct...that's exactly right. It's the wink from across the room. The goal is to get your attention and to get you to give me your email address. Then, our follow-up email program is really like a relationship-building system. Sometimes we talk on the phone, and sometimes we may meet and work on our goals together. We say that our goal is to get our customers to like

137

us, and we try to get them interested in what we have to offer so they'll buy from us. Hopefully, by building this relationship, they will buy from us and continue to buy from us.

Yes, and doing this it doesn't have to be a huge event. I am not a computer guy. Doug knows more about it then me. All you need to know how to do is to hook up with the right people who know how to get this stuff out there.

Sometimes you hear people say that they don't have time. I know that is where a lot of my frustrations came from. in the beginning. I was talking to a hundred different people, but I was spinning my wheels and never put any deals together because I wasn't zeroing in on my target market.

Not only that, but if you talk to every person that calls you about little stuff, you'll use up all of your time that way. You have to value your time and protect it, which will mean putting some people off and not talking to them...that was hard to do, but has made a huge difference.

The best thing you can do is to concentrate on and zero in on your target market. When I did my $19 million in sales, I only had 700 people on my email list, so that is why I say you need to zero in on what you want. You don't need to have a big, massive list to do business. Now, if you have a bigger list, then, yes, you will do more business, but you just need it to get started.

That is where it all starts at...just one. And not just in real estate, it's in anything you do. You've got to get it going...do that first one,

whatever that is for you. You start it, tweak it, work it, tweak it again and keep on going.

I read several different papers every day. That's where I get my information from that I give to my list. By them getting that information from me, it keeps them interested.

What people have to remember is that it's a relationship-building process. It's just like everything else...it takes time. You're not going to get rich overnight, but, in time, you could be very comfortable.

Right. We're not always trying to sell things ...we also educate and inform people of events that are going on. By building my list, and keeping it growing...in my mind, that's a continuous sales pitch, so that when any of my 5,000 people on my email list decide to buy a condo, they will think of me first. They'll think, "He is the pre-construction condo man. He has been nice enough to send us all the information that we needed and asked for, so let's go to him." That's why sometimes we will send out multiple emails a day with different bits of information. We don't expect to get anything in return – they don't have to buy anything – but we hope they remember us when they want to.

Something else people have to remember is that if you don't make some people mad, then you're not doing your job. Have you ever sent out an email and gotten a response back from one or more of your readers that was negative?

Yes. Every once in a while, I will get an

email back telling me it was a stupid article, you're full of bologna, etc. That used to really bother me, in the beginning, but then I learned to push the delete button and delete them off my list. Occasionally, we will email back and forth to each other voicing our opinion on things...nothing mean or nasty, just to have a nice little debate. But, overall, if they are obnoxious – I just push delete and they're gone.

People like that are just miserable people, and that's what they live for. They are miserable in their own life, and they try to bring others down to their level. So, you don't want to force situations when there really isn't anything there. That goes for real estate too.
I think a lot of people, especially in the beginning, try to force a deal through...they are trying to force a buyer or a seller to go along with them, but some of your best deals may be the deals that you never do.

You know me, Mark, I'm not a hard sale kind of guy. I'm not a slick New York car salesman kind of guy. I'm a pretty easygoing guy, conservative, slow-talking guy. I think my success in sales is because I have always delivered to my people honesty, integrity, enthusiasm and a passion for what I am doing. Mostly, though, just good information about what I'm doing.

That is what it takes to make customers come back. I know the kind of people that I want to work with and vise-versa. I want to work with people that are willing to accept 100% responsibility for their life – good decisions or

140

bad.

We can all say yes or no to anything in life, but a lot of successful people take full responsibility and move on and focus on the good, not the bad decisions. Don't get me wrong, there are times when you may want to blame others, but...when it all comes down to it, it's on you.

I don't really have any complaints anymore because I continue to keep up good communication with them. I don't try to BS them at all. I give honest and valid information. But, more importantly, I try to be pro-active and give them the information that I think they might be thinking about.

That's why I will take pictures of these condos while they are under construction and send them out before they even ask for them. I got an email this morning asking me for some pictures, and I found that odd because I usually get pictures out before anyone ever asks for them. So, now I look at it like I was running a little behind, and I should have had that done a couple of weeks ago.

Well, that's because you're too busy sitting on your patio and enjoying the lake. That's the problem, Doug.

Yeah, that's it. And I really do want to be able to do that – that's part of my goal.

I'm sure you will find a way to do that in the most effortlessly way, and I think this is what it all comes down to.

So, get the first deal under your belt. You

are going to be scared and nervous. You're not going to know exactly what to say or how to say it. When you say it, just be you, and let it come together. Just by doing that, things will start coming together effortlessly...everything will begin to fall into place just like it was meant to be.

Just get out and do something.

Yes. You will get a whole lot more done by doing *something* instead of nothing.

I have customers that ask me several different questions about everything we send out...and these guys have never bought anything. Every single time, they ask multiple questions about properties we are offering, and then they disappear. Then, I have to get after them because they are spinning their wheels...and my wheels ...and we aren't accomplishing anything.

Just make a decision, stick with it and move on. That is what building a business is all about. If you're sitting there hem-hawing over a $20 expense instead of spending $1,000 to watch your business grow, I really don't see how you *can* grow. Anybody I know that is successful makes a decision, sticks with it, moves on and re-works it if it wasn't the right decision. Once again, taking the C+ to the A+. You don't know until you do it, right? Just getting it up and going...we can always correct situations and keep moving forward...it's called progressing.

That's right.

Doug, are there any kinds of closing things that you would like to talk about?

Yes. I think it is important, like we talked about earlier, to move forward one step at a time. Don't expect to go from step A to step Z in one step. You have to go through the whole process... climb every rung on the ladder. You've got to get it started.

So, if you can run a little bit, skip or just pass one up here and there, that's ok, but you've got to work through the process. The key is to just get up and get to doing something every day. If you have a 9 to 5 job, and your goal is to be a real estate investor, then you have got to do something related to real estate every single day. I don't care if it is reading an article in the paper, driving by a house or whatever – do something... be involved and learn.

Exactly. That's the whole thing. You have got to get out there, and you have to be consistent...you have to keep it going. Don't do it once, and that's it. You have to keep doing it over and over and over again. As you do that, your daily consistent actions will supersede any kind of intelligence because it's all about numbers and repetition.

Keep that positive outlook. Keep surrounding yourself with positive people like Doug, myself and other people that are do-ers and not talkers ...that is another key too.

Well, Doug, I do appreciate your time. Where can people find your website? What's the address?

The website address is: www.dougdoebler.com.

Excellent. Thanks, again, Doug. Everyone, you need to get on his list because he is making things happen.

Goodbye, Mark.

Bye!

"Courage is not the lack of fear. It is acting in spite of it."

- Mark Twain; Author

Chapter Five
Interview with Paul Strauss

Paul Strauss is a highly successful, serial entrepreneur and a real estate investor from the Chicago, Illinois area. He's also a Managing Member of Yes Investors, LLC and Founder and President of www.WCRT.org, one of the fastest growing associations of entrepreneurial real estate investors in the country. He's been an active real estate investor for five years, and he's been a full-time investor since 2002. This guy's got a lot of stuff going on, so you need to have a pen and paper ready to take notes.

If you've got kids running around, you need to have a babysitter or have someone watch them, shut the door. I really want you to dive into this and understand this. I don't want you to miss any piece of this. You're very luck to now have this in your library so you can go back through it over and over and over.

Welcome aboard, Paul.

Thank you Mark. Thanks for having me.

Excellent. So, I said you're a serial entrepreneur and that you've been doing this for five years, and you've been a full-time investor since 2002. Give a quick overview of where you came from, you know, what your background is and how you got to managing what you're doing now.

145

I was doing the same thing everybody else did. When I got out of high school, I decided that I needed to go to college. My parents weren't prepared to foot the bill, and I didn't really want to borrow a bunch of money, so I joined the Navy. I went in September of '89 and got out precisely in September of '93 and utilized my GI bill to go to school.

I did that and started working hard and earning a decent living, nothing special. I always had something going on the side because my number one job never paid me enough to do some of the things I wanted to do like travel and buy some of the things I wanted to buy to enjoy myself.

So, I did what a lot of people do, I worked harder. I went out and got myself a job, in the form of a business, working hard and making things happen. I ran a landscaping business for a lot of years on the side. I called it "beer and pizza money". If it weren't for that job, we would have never taken a trip and would have probably never had anything in our savings, you know?

It's one of those things that I just did. I had cut grass since I was in high school because I never did work a "regular" job back then like many high school kids – you know, retail, fast food, what have you. Instead, I did odd jobs for the neighbors by cleaning up their yards and things like that. I was making more money than all my friends that had jobs so that was an early "clue".

I came back to Illinois from Georgia after I got out of the Navy. I got a job...a series of jobs, really...and ended up in the financial services

146

industry with a very well known investment/ financial institution.

Around 1999, somebody tried to recruit me for a multi-level business, I know that some of you have been in multi-level businesses and done those things. I have nothing against it, but, at the time, it certainly wasn't for me. I said "no" to the opportunity, but this guy gave me a book to read. He said, "Look, I understand that you're not going to do this business, but you need to read this book because it will change your life and your mindset. Once you do that, you'll make a fortune no matter what you do." The book he gave me was called *Rich Dad Poor Dad* by Robert Kiyosaki.

Paul, if you don't mind me stopping you there.

No, go ahead.

I think the big importance in that, Paul, is giving value even if there's nothing there. Don't you think by just building that value, like you said, it's opened your eyes to a whole new world? Well, this is why you're talking to me now, right?

Exactly. You can trace it back to that. That book just opened my eyes. It said a lot of things that I knew, intuitively. If you think about what very wealthy people do, a lot of them work very hard, but they also work very smart. One of the things that you will not find ultra-wealthy people doing are the mundane details of what they produce. They are masters at delegating- at allocating labor and capital, and they do those

147

two things very well.

If you want to make a lot of money, you need to become a master at allocating labor and capital. From that book, I learned that working harder and earning more money was just trading more hours for more dollars, and there was a limit to that. It was the first time I'd ever thought about that.

I don't know how many people have heard of Paulie Sabol or Donna Fox, but they wrote a great book called "From Credit Repair to Credit Millionaire" and were in the Northwest Indiana area investing in real estate, along with some other guys named David Culver, and Ryan Steele that came along side of me to help me out. Basically, I did this...I ran full-force into doing several deals, and, by that, I mean buying properties.

Paul, you're getting ready to get into your story, but before we get too deep, though, what he's talking about is going around and gathering the people that are doing it and not just talking about it.

The people we're talking about are do-ers. You don't want to go to places where everybody is just standing around acting like they're doing something. At the places and events we're talking about, you'll find mentors there as well as mentors in the making.

It's the relentless, forward motion of going out and finding that person that can help you get to the next level. Like he said, "Successful people surround themselves around these people all day long." How can I do better delegation? Find the delegation expert. How can I do better with finances? Find a financial expert. Find people to

148

align yourself with that you know that can take you to the next level that you want to get to. Your mentors will change as you grow...it's just part of the process.

And you'll outgrow some of your mentors.

Good mentors want you to outgrow them. This is like being a parent and saying you want your children to be better than you. Mentors understand that and value that...that's what they want for you. They want to help you get to the next level because they see their own achievements through helping you to reach your dreams, and they want you to grow past what they've achieved. And, let's face it, they can shave off so many years by helping you take the next step.

Right. And you want to look for a mentor that is really of that mindset. You want to look for a mentor that's really looking out for you. There are a lot of people out there calling themselves mentors that are really just trying to squeeze another nickel out of you. And if we can just be real for a second...there's a lot of crap out there.

Exactly. The thing is...what I said before... that's what there needs to be more of. A mentor should tell you what you *need* to hear, not what you *want* to hear — your mentors need to be real people that are out there doing it, not just talking about it.

Don't get me wrong. There are some great people that can talk it and show people how to do it, but they just aren't good at the day to day of it. Finding that right mentor...it's a process.

149

If you don't have someone you can compare it against, what's a good mentor?

In the beginning, find someone you feel comfortable with that has already reached the level where you want to be. Also, be sure you find out who your mentors' mentors are. Who have they and who *are* they learning from? You don't want someone that has stopped learning and thinks they have all the answers.

Any good mentor knows that he doesn't have all the answers, but what he does know is that he has a rolodex, and he knows the person to call.

What we want to do now is talk about how to really go out there and take some action. We're going to talk about Paul's first couple of deals, and why it was so important for him to get off the fence and take massive action. So, Paul, do you want to discuss, and I know a little bit about this story and everything, but let's just shine the light and rock and roll, I guess on this and show them what's going on.

Sure. Now, I don't want to get off track, but I do want to talk quickly about a talk show interview I saw recently. The person being interviewed was born without fully developed arms and legs, and he's written a book about his life and overcoming his obstacles.

He actually became a college wrestler. His only goal, when he started, was not to ever be pinned. In the course of over a year and a half, he lost 35 wrestling matches, but he never once thought about quitting.

150

When I heard that, I thought, "Wow, I'm about to do an interview with Mark and lie about my first two deals." That really hit home, listening to what he had to say about persistence. It never occurred to him that he wouldn't eventually win... it just never occurred to him.

I think you have to have that attitude, and that's the attitude that I had when I started out. I knew what I didn't want. I knew that I didn't want to work another 40 or 50 years kicking into a social security system that would never kick anything back out, and working very hard for other people and living like a pauper so that I could exist after retirement and take care of myself.

Let's be real too. If you're not an entrepreneur, and you're not a business owner, you can still do well, financially. You will just have to live below your means and you will have to save a lot. You will do very little other than save and count pennies and things like that. But, you *can* do well, financially, and build security for yourself if you're willing to knuckle down and live with those parameters I just mentioned, which I was not willing to do.

Parameters and making that decision. I study a lot of wealthy people. I've also been lucky enough to get around great mentors and have great mentors in my life because I took action on that side of it because I knew that's what it would take. But to take that action and stick with it, where you know nothing's going to stop you... it is so key. And when you make that decision, there's nothing that *can* stop you!

You don't have to get it right the first time. My mentor always said, "Mark, you don't have

to get it right, you just have to get it going." I know that this interview is going to impact a lot of people that are faced with what we're talking about. This is a huge problem in real estate investing...everybody getting ready to get ready and letting this happen over and over.

Planning to plan.

Exactly. It's a silent killer. Not just in real estate, but in any business and in life as well. You need to take *action*. If you've got it on your mind, and you have the right people around you, there's no way you won't succeed. Is it going to be tough? Absolutely. But, with determination and persistence and relentless forward motion, you can't stop. It's just not even possible to fail.

Exactly. And I think that's what I decided on. I started knowing what I didn't want, but then I continued knowing what I *would* have, regardless of the cost. I knew that there was a price to be paid for success. I counted it, and I decided that it was something I was willing to pay for.

In November, 2002, the company I was working for decided they no longer needed my services. So, I was standing in line getting ready to go to a second job interview, and one of the requirements for that was going to take a drug test. So, I'm in the bathroom with a woman that's about 7 feet tall looking over my shoulder while I'm doing my thing in a little cup, right? At that point, I just decided that my life had become ridiculous. So, I went home, and I talked to my wife about this.

She asked me, "Well, ok, if you're going to do this, how long is it going to take?" I said, "I want to tell you two things from the get-go: 1) I don't know how long it's going to take and 2) I don't even know if I'm going to make it. But I do know one thing about continuing on this new path we're on...we'll be ok."

There's a couple things Paul touched on that people need to understand. First, is that it *will* all be ok. It's not the end of the world if you fail. You *will* have failures, but you're not going to fail, overall. Just keep moving forward.

One thing that I can say is that the wealthy understand that money makes money. Being around these successful people, I learned that very early on. What they do is they take the majority of what they earn and they put it back into their businesses to keep them growing...they're constantly reinvesting in themselves because they know *that* will make all the difference in the long-run.

There's a saying out there that "if you want to double your income, go get another full-time job" (laughing), but that's not it at all. Let's face it, wealthy people just "get" it...don't work for money, have money working for you.

Benjamin Franklin said, "Money makes money and the money-maker makes money." For me, that's the money you want to live on. The rest of that money, you want to go find a use for, and put it to work for you.

I think that's one mistake that people who do succeed make in real estate...they start spending that money they earn from wholesaling instead of investing it into other avenues that will pay them for life. Wholesaling is really just a job. You need to become an investor in your future... you need to think about putting that money to work.

Exactly. And the thing is that you can do both.

Paul, one part of the business that I do a lot of and that I love is wholesaling. I love wholesaling because I just love being involved in that side of it. I understand that that's what best fits my business model...versus doing rehabs, for instance. Rehabs no longer fit into my business model. Other people's business models might include retailing, rehabbing, wholesaling, pre-foreclosures, etc. or any combination of those, but it's important to know what the best model is for what you're trying to accomplish.

The great thing is that the kinds of people I want to interview and bring to you, the people who are reading this, are people that have different flavors. Everybody has a personality. Everybody has their own lifestyle that they want to create or live, etc. and their own ways of getting there. That's why I like to bring different flavors. I don't want it to just be me, and you only see one side of it. I want you to see the full picture. Paul loves buying and holding, but I'm a terrible property manager, and I know that.

I like wholesaling too, Mark. We've made a pretty good business of wholesaling properties and rehabbing. We've actually done quite a bit of rehabbing. In fact, the first couple of deals I'm going to talk about...one of the reasons I lost

154

money is because I'm a pretty darn good rehabber and went overboard. What happened is that I rehabbed the dickens out of the first place!

The thing I wanted to emphasize is that no matter what you do to bring in that cash, you've got to put that money towards something. Whether that means holding the property or whether that means buying notes and putting paper on properties (you can make a pretty penny that way too).

These are all great areas that he's talking about. Paul, lets go ahead and get started and talk about your first couple of deals and how it went totally opposite from what you thought it would. And then, how you corrected it as quickly as possible to just keep moving forward.

Well, I got a hold of a property, so I was calling up my mentors like, "Hey, do you have a contract for a property?" He's like, "How do you want to do the deal?" I said, "Well, I think maybe I'm doing a lease option but I don't know. I've got to get back and talk to the seller. They just want to sell me this property, and I've got to get it and..."

I wasn't really paying attention, so what we ended up doing was I ended up putting the property under contract and brought another guy in for the financing because I didn't have a strong enough income statement, at that time, to buy it myself. My credit was ok but it was a debt to income issue, so I brought this guy in as a partner.

I was pretty confident that I could rehab a house. I don't know if any of you have seen

155

the movie "*The Money Pit*." Yeah, well, I grew up there. So, I figured that I knew how to do this. This was my life, you know – gutting a house and repairing it. I grew up in the "money pit" house with my Dad, so I could figure this out pretty well, and I did it.

I did it in a working-class neighborhood that I was unfamiliar with, and we rehabbed the dickens out of the place. It was a complete rehab job. I found out later that what I should have done was carpeted and painted the thing, sold it and been done with it. What we did is we over-improved and put a price on the property that we thought was fair, based on all the work that we had done.

What I learned, at that point, is that you will get the price for the property that the market will bare. Just because you spent $3,000 on countertops doesn't mean that you get to add $3,000 to your bottom line. Some of you are thinking, "Well that's common sense." But there are people reading this that don't know that...I certainly didn't know it when I started out.

Paul, we run across this everyday. This is a big common question, "How do I rehab...how much do I put into it?" There's so many pieces. I don't do a whole lot of rehabs anymore. I've done a bunch. I just don't like dealing with contractors anymore.

For me, it ended up being glorified babysitting. There are all these different people doing different parts of the job, but you have to depend on them to all do what they're supposed to do when they're supposed to do it. I mean, you can't have your drywall guy come in until the

156

electrician's done, so if the electrician doesn't live up to his end of the bargain, you can see how it throw off the schedule for the rest of the job...the drywaller, the painter, the carpeters, etc. There are "good eggs" out there, but it just didn't fit into my business model anymore.

Paul, can you give us a tip or two of what to look for when you're rehabbing a house so that you know what your end-buyers will be looking for and won't over-improve?

Go and look at For Sale houses in the marketplace that you're going to, and then talk to local Realtors and find out what they're emphasizing and you'll get a pretty good idea of what to do and not do where rehabbing is concerned.

And when he says "emphasizing", he means amenities like the siding (what colors are they using?), carpets/flooring (are they putting stone on the fireplace?), etc. Just see what the common thread is in the area and mimic what the big developers/builders are doing. If you do it that way, you won't over-improve a property, which will force you to put a higher price tag on it, which could make it harder to sell.

Also, go look for all the major Realtor/Agent signs in the neighborhoods. Then, go tour them when they're doing Open Houses on Sundays from noon to 4 just to see what the Realtor is talking about and pointing out. You'll get a pretty good idea of what the market is looking for because Realtors are just trying to meet their clients' needs. They're trying to emphasize what's positive about the property but, more importantly, they're kind of showing you the key features that you're going to need to have in your rehabbed house as well.

If you go through a house and you notice that there are no granite countertops in the $150,000 house price-range, well, that's called a "clue", so don't put granite countertops in a house in that price-range. By the same token, if you're trying to sell a $660,000 penthouse condo in the suburbs that is close to the metro in the Chicago area, don't try to sell that property by throwing down a sheet of vinyl in the kitchen and putting in laminate countertops because it just won't sell.

You kind of have to know what your buyers are looking for because, ultimately, all you really need to do is: a) find out what people want, b) go get it and c) give it to them. No matter what business you're in, if you can remember those three things, you'll do very well. Your clients are your end-buyers regardless of whether it's a rehabber that you're going to wholesale the property to or whether it's a retail buyer who will buy it from you on a Rent To Own.

Could you go ahead and give some numbers on your first deal? How you found it, how you bought it and all the different parts of the deal. Keep in mind that this is a deal he did in the Chicago area, correct, Paul?

Yes, just outside of Chicago.

So, if you're in California or in another hot market where the houses go for a million dollars, just add a zero to what he's talking about...there's no difference.

This property is in a neighborhood that I actually haven't been back to since then because, early on, I didn't really own what I did wrong... I blamed it on the market. Basically, it was a working-class neighborhood. The house was a little ranch, with about 1,200 square feet. Like I said, I had a money partner on the deal, and I was the project manager.

I didn't know what a "comp" was when I started this project...it might have helped a little bit if I had. The highest comp in the area was about $186,000. To give you an idea of where my head was at, I was thinking $205,000 to $210,000. Because, again, I'm referring back to my own market. I'm referring back to what I know (or think I know). I'm saying to myself, "At $210,000, that's a cheap house" because in *my* market the medium home price is $355,000.

So, to go to this low-income, working-class neighborhood, that's a cheap house for somebody. Somebody would buy that house at that price. At the time, I didn't know there were a lot of little neighborhoods where you could get a house like that and still be within 50 miles of Chicago. I'm thinking, "This is cheap. This is great! I ought to move here. It's cheap to live here."

We picked it up for $179,000, which is about retail for the property. We put around $13,000 into it via improvements. Now we're right up there at our market, but we're still thinking we can make a buck. We ended up selling that house for about what houses sell for in that area. We sold it for right around, $191,000 or something close to that.

And was it listed with a Realtor, Paul?

Yeah, it was...with a discount broker, but we still had to pay 2%. So, we took a bath on the house. We basically paid a Realtor out of our own pockets because, mind you, there we're carrying cost too, that added to that loss I'm talking about.

Absolutely.

That cost is thrown in those rehab numbers, but that's the number that doesn't stop. If any of you know who Frank McKinney is, he tells you that if you want to know what a property's going to cost you to carry, go crank up all the lights and the air conditioning and go outside and look at the electric meter. He says that for every minute that you own that house, just envision that happening. Those are the costs that are eating you. You've got to get it marketed and sold...yesterday. Frank is a master of marketing. At this point, though, we were in the panic stage. We had become the seller that we were originally looking for!

So, you were starting to become a motivated seller?

Exactly. We *were* the motivated seller. We just did not want to make another mortgage payment on this property. That was our whole motivation for the last 30 days that we owned that house. We just kept saying, "Lord, please don't make us make another mortgage payment on this house."

When the numbers shook out, we lost

about $7,000 on the deal, but when the dust cleared, we'd really lost about $8,200 on that property, overall.

Paul, about the timeframe from start to finish to get to the loss of the $8,200 – what kind of timeframe was that, and what was going on? It wasn't just because the market was slow...it was also because the house was over-improved and over-priced...

We took a long time to do that rehab. We owned the property for four months before we ever put a "For Sale" sign up in the front yard. That was another mistake. Now in my contracts, I write, "Seller agrees that buyer will put a "For Sale" or "For Rent" sign on the property upon acceptance of the contract." There are house that I don't even own right now (but that are under contract), and they have a "For Sale" sign out front because I learned that lesson. – don't wait!

I've since really learned it from Frank – you need to make a big deal out of your property that you're going to sell outright to a retail buyer (this will be different for the ones that you're going to wholesale. You make a big deal about it to all of your network. I know that Mark can talk a lot about that because he's got an awesome buyers' list for all of you that are wholesalers out there.

So, there was about a four month timeframe in which we owned that house, and we were into our fifth month when we finally sold it. Like I said, we were almost <u>done</u> with the rehab process before it ever occurred to us to run ads and/or put a "For Sale" sign out...huge mistake that cost us a lot of time and money.

161

This is a common problem, Paul. You're just so focused on getting it done, sometimes, that everything else slips away.

And, coming from the financial services industry, I'm not "wired right" for marketing anyway...but, I am now, believe me! What ended up happening was I was like, "Ok, well, you *step one*: buy the house, then *step two*: you fix up the house, then *step three*: when it's all fixed up, then you sell the property...right?

I mean, you don't want people looking at it before it's done, do you? You don't want a "For Sale" sign out there...you don't want people to see it in this condition. I had no idea how wrong I was.

I didn't know that...didn't know that it would be ok for people to see it before it's 100% done. I didn't know that you might want to start out advertising it as a "handyman special" and then move into a seller-financing deal and then, finally, to retail. It will sell via one of these avenues, so you have to find which ones works for you for that particular deal.

So, Paul, that was your first deal. Now let's talk about that some more because what you just said was very key to success. You gave three different examples of how to sell this same exact property in different "stages of production". How key is *that* to your business today?

Our basic process is like this: from the moment we have it under contract, it's for sale. Everything that we have is for sale at the right

162

price...well, except my wife and kid. Once we have the contract signed, an advertisement for the property goes out to our rehabber network, and we try to get the property sold that way while we're still working on it. It's also being marketed as a "handyman special". Recognizing that one way of selling may not work every time, we'll start here and change it up as needed.

Once we get to the point where it only needs some cosmetic work, we'll offer seller-financing. That's where we put our focus/emphasis on our marketing and on seller-financing because then we can exit by targeting a wannabe homeowner and do a lease option or a land contact. You may even get lucky in that the person moving in will be willing to complete the work needed and save you from having that extra out of pocket expense. I don't like doing these as well, though, because I don't like paying my taxes on day one.

If you haven't done a land contract yet, talk to your accountant, and he'll tell you all about what a land contract is. Now, I'm not an accountant or a lawyer, but it's my understanding that the property is considered sold _that day_, and you pay taxes on it as if it sold that day.

Then the final stage, if it's going to be a retail property, it's a pretty typical retail sale. We do list them...I have nothing against listing agents, but I'd rather not pay their commissions if I can help it. So that's kind of our stages of production.

Ok, so on the first deal you lost $8,200 but, yet, you gained five months of experience through that process.... how important, Paul, was that five months to you?

It was like five months of college, but better than college, actually. I learned more in less time and for less money than in any other point in my life.

And that's a great point too. I'm just trying to show people that when you got yourself in those shoes and now you're facing that $8,200 loss what are you thinking? What was your thought process at that point...give up, go home? Or now that I know what _not_ to do, I'll just push forward and then do it again but not make the same mistakes...right?

There's that, and there's sleep with one eye open because my wife is going to kill me (laughing). At that time, everything was held jointly with my other partner, but it was *his* name that was on the mortgage of that property, not mine. He'd also had to come out of pocket to pay the real estate commissions just like I had. So, when I say $8,200 – that was the total portion of *my* loss. I don't manage projects anymore, so I don't worry about all this as much as I used to, but I still think about that lesson.

The other thing that was going through my mind is that we needed to do another deal because we've got to make this up. You know, we've got to make some money...but after six months, we still hadn't found another deal yet.

I mean, my credit cards were maxed at ridiculously high interest rates. Another huge financing mistake we made was that we bought everything we needed on day one with those credit cards at various home improvement stores.

Only buy your materials and whatever else when you actually need it. Believe me, the stuff you need to get the job done will still be there in a month, so there's no hurry to go spend the cash until you absolutely have to.

That is so key, Paul. I've seen so many people getting started think that they have to go out and get the LLC setup, they have to have all these asset protection plans in place, etc. but the thing is that until you have assets to protect and have started making money, none of that matters. The same goes for buying materials for a rehab project. If you need a box of nails today, go get them, but don't buy 12 boxes because you might need that cash for something else tomorrow, but now it's gone, and you just have to go spend more.

And we did. So, it was either go get a job and pay this all back...I don't know if you all have ever made credit card payments, but it takes more than a little while to pay $8,200 off. I wasn't interested in that plan, so we needed to find another deal.

About that time was when I started meeting with the people who would eventually mentor me. I met several of them through online discussion boards. In fact, I still post on them every once in a while. My team was kind of starting to come together and people were giving me different options about what to do about the situation.

My partner and I ended up partnering with another guy on a rehab property because we'd had that rehab experience, and we could see that he was about to do the same thing. We

165

said, "Hey, come here. Let's talk about this." He said, "Alright. If you'll help me on this, we'll split everything." That property was in another, similar neighborhood, but we knew a lot more now. We bought that one right and did ok with it in the end.

Ok, so you lost on the first deal. The second deal...you didn't want to go through that long plan of paying a credit card back through a job because that's not in your plan, of course, right? You took the next step and did a joint venture and now you're up to the plate again. Did you profit off that deal?

I did. We made about $12,300 on that deal. If you take everything from the first deal into account, though, I didn't really make any money. I had that to take care of, along with my partners, and I also had to cover my living expenses for that time period. So, when you figure it all out...I made all this money, and it looked like a big check on the HUD (closing statement), but when the profit got split up, I was pretty much at break-even.

The thing with that, though, Paul, let's just say that you didn't make any money during that twelve month period. How important is it, though...there's no way you can gain that kind of experience by reading a book or going to a seminar, right?

Absolutely. Doing those two properties was the best damn boot camp I ever went to. As much as a good coach or mentor or boot camp will try to teach you, you can't learn this stuff on a bus ride looking at properties out a window. You've really got to get in there, and you've really got to put yourself out there and just take a chance. You've just got to take action.

If you've learned from some of the things I talked about...awesome, that was the point. Hopefully, you won't make some of the really obvious mistakes that I made. I know some investors are listening to this saying, "Ha ha... well, that's obvious...I knew that". Well, I didn't at the time.

It's only obvious if you know about it, right?

Yeah, and I sure know about it now. We watch comps, but here's another "magic number" that you need to know...the time on market, how long a house has been for sale. Don't start a rehab in June if your time on market is 123 days, which it was in this neighborhood, because you will still own that thing in October. Imagine trying to sell in Chicago in the winter. Not only have all the kids gone back to school and nobody wants to move, but it gets dark at two o'clock in the afternoon! It's hard to see that the house is even for sale, let alone see the property from the street.

These are the kinds of things you have to know and think about. You have to think about the "end", the end of your project. You know, one of those "Seven Habits..." you hear about that tells you to "begin with the end in mind". I think better of some of those decisions now. I think about the end. I think about where am I going to be...where and what is my exit?

It's not the "getting" that's the hard part. I know there are a lot of new investors that think getting the deal is the hard part. No, it's getting rid of the deal that will be your challenge. It's getting a tenant in there, it's getting it sold, it's getting it wholesaled. A guy I heard speak the other weekend said, "It's a whole lot easier to find a house for a buyer than it is to find a buyer for a house." Simple statement, but it's true. Go find out what people want. Go get it, and then give it to them.

You need to be taking notes here. The stuff he's saying might sound obvious, but a lot of it _is_ so obvious that you just don't do it. I've been guilty of this. I still am guilty of, "Ok, yeah I know that, but why did I just miss it on the last deal?" All these pieces are key...these are golden nuggets that you can take and implement tomorrow into your business.

He said something, though, that I want to stress...see how long properties sit on the market in your target area. Another confusing factor for people, though, is not just the days on market, Paul. You hear people say, "Well, the properties are listed for $150,000." Ok, that's great and everything, but what is the _sold price_ of those properties?

Yes...you must look at sold comps...nothing else is a true comp.

Yes, there is a big difference in sold comps as opposed to the listing price. Think of it this way, you can go in and over-improve a house and put it on the market for $175,000 but if it's in a

neighborhood where nothing is selling for more than $150,000 you're just not going to get that price.

If you put in $30,000 of landscaping and a state of the art kitchen with all the bells and whistles, but you're the *only* one in the neighborhood that's done that, there's nothing to compare your house to, so the value that you feel like you've added just won't show up in what the house will actually sell for. I've seen homeowners do it so many times...I feel bad for them, but they just don't understand how the markets work.

A comp is taking other, similar houses, in a small radius that have most of the same amenities and averaging all of their recent sales prices. So, in any given neighborhood, every 2-story, 3 bedroom house with a basement and a 2-car garage is going to sell for about the same price. So, the guy that put in $30,000 of landscaping is going to have to eat that because his house will still just sell for the $150,000 like every other one in that neighborhood.

If a Realtor ever comes to you and says, "You can buy this place for $400,000 and easily sell it for $650,000" the first question is usually, "So, why don't you buy it?" And, really, there are legitimate answers to that question, but there are also B.S. answers to that question. The B.S. answer is to dodge it all together and say, "Well, I'm really focused on this right now," or "I don't do that right now".

Or there's the legitimate answer of, "Well, it needs about $120,000 in work." There's some people...heck, I'll do $120,000 worth of work, but there's some people that won't. I would do that

169

amount of work for $100,000+ profit. We'll take that deal, and we'll get it done.

Paul you said something too. This is a huge problem to some people, and a concern that they face everyday — people who are brand new to investing or even people that have been in the business. The "problem" that I'm talking about is the age old question of, "How do I find deals? You guys act like it so easy."

To me, it *is* simple. To you...I know you talk about how easy it is. Can you just give some pointers or ideas, tricks, strategies...whatever... to get these people to go get some deals. Let's get them to their first deal quicker, easier, and less painfully.

The first deal, I'm telling you...it's so key to your success. People spend thousands of dollars on boot camps, but they hardly ever go do a deal afterwards. They spend all weekend hearing about how exciting it is and how "easy" it is, and they leave that weekend all pumped up...but then it dies off once they get home and they're out of that environment.

See, this is where the power of a mentor comes in. There is no accountability for the average person leaving a boot camp to go home and make it happen...no one who's going to follow up with you to make sure you do what you need to do. A mentor will call you on Monday morning and be like "Ok, what are you going to do today with all that you learned. Let's put together an action plan that you can implement now to move forward."

Paul, let's give some tips and strategies on what you do, specifically, to find your sellers.

Sellers are people and people go where people go. Our kind of systematic auto-pilot way of finding and contracting sellers is what we've found to be the best way. We subscribe to a couple of public data services that get legal notices on mortgage defaults...and there are probably a half a dozen of these services where you live, if not more.

Some of the services will give you just raw data. Most counties have this data available online. If you Google your county's Sheriff's foreclosure list, you can most likely find that list...it's public, and it's out there.

What we do is, we mail postcards to those lists. It's just auto-pilot, every two weeks...we don't even think about it. There are online services that will print you postcards, print your labels and include postage. That's kind of our auto-pilot thing, and the responses to those postcards goes to a voicemail system that we have, or you can direct people to a website.

I think it's very important if you don't have a website, to get a website. I don't think anything does less for your credibility than to go and talk to a homeowner about their biggest asset...what they think is their biggest asset, anyway... You're talking to them about their home, their property that's worth several hundred thousand dollars, and you're email address is: ibuyhouses123@yahoo.com. Go get a website name. At the very least, make sure you have a respectable email address like paul@offerin12hours.com. When you have a website, it just gives you that much more credibility when you talk to people.

171

I mean, I realize that I'm just Paul who buys houses, but I recognize that I have an image too, which is whatever I put it out there to be. People will either see you as credible or not, so it's your choice as to how you're perceived.

So, I have a website. I have a dedicated phone number that my wife and kids will not answer. We have a professional voicemail system. We have things like this that do not cost a lot of money. Some of you think it is really expensive, but in reality you're losing more by not having it.

If you're going to market, you need to be credible when you do that, and people need to see you as somebody they can talk to about their house...someone that they can trust. If you have a nice job, God bless you, and if you have a nice car, God bless you even more, but you've really got to be careful pulling up to somebody's house in a BMW when they're about to go into foreclosure.

We had a wholesaling class a couple weeks ago, and one of the speakers said that he actually went up to a woman's house, was talking to her about her house, and she said...and I quote, "Where you car at?" He said, "It's right over there." He was driving a Honda Civic, and she said, "Alright, I'll talk to you." That stuck in my head. I never really thought about it until that point. I don't drive a fancy car or anything like that...I'm just not a car person. I drive my Toyota pickup truck that I've been driving forever.

The thing is, be careful of the impression that you give people. Be professional, but not slick. Be well-spoken, but not too well-spoken because guys in suits are the ones that they think are trying to take away their house, right?

Exactly. I just want to explain this. You don't have to be super polished, just be yourself. I talk about this a lot. Don't try to be me, don't try to be Paul, don't try to be anybody but yourself. When you go in and you're faking it, that's when you're going to get labeled as "slick" salesman for no reason. Just be you.

If they ask you a question that you don't know the answer to, just say, "I don't know, but let me ask my partner." It's these little things that help to not give anybody false hope. If you can help them, you can. If you can't, let them know and move on.

And don't worry if you're in a situation where you really need for a deal to happen, like Paul was in his first deal. The minute you feel yourself "chasing" a deal, walk away...in the long-run it will be the best move you make. Making a deal happen where there isn't one or where it isn't a win/win for everyone is never a good thing, trust me.

It's always taken to extremes, it seems. Don't be a charitable foundation, but don't be a shark either. You just have to find a niche where you really care about helping people. If you don't care about people right now, may I suggest that you develop a heart for people...if you're going to make it in this business, that is.

That's all this business really is — it's nothing more than relationship-building. Once I started focusing on the buyers and sellers, I started seeing the biggest growth to my business, and it's been booming ever since.

173

I was going to say that nothing will make a distressed seller happier than if you just tell them, "I'm sorry, but I can't help you" rather than string them along and tell them two weeks later. These people do not have time to wait around for you... that's the one thing they're out of. The clock is ticking, and that's just not fair.

Have some integrity about putting your name on the line. If you put your name on a contract and your intention is that, if you can't sell it, you're not going to close it, then tell them that. It's ok, really. Tell them, "This is what I'm going to try to do...find a buyer for your house, or find someone to help me close on it, etc." Give them the option that it's ok if they continue trying to sell it. You're looking for a buyer too, so whichever happens first is ok. Don't stick them in a contract and say, "Well, I've got the contract, and you can't sell it to anybody else" and/or threaten to sue them if they do. Something stupid like that will haunt you later on. Just do people right. Don't do anything you couldn't explain to your Mom.

Treat others as you would want to be treated. Like Paul said, these people are out of time. Time is what they don't have...nor do they have money. Not only that, but every investor is coming to them like prey in the middle of the desert. They're just picking at these people waiting for them to fall on their face...making false promises, etc. I'm not talking about all of them, but there are a lot of them.

Today – and this is no joke – I was sitting in my house talking to this lady, and she was like, "Can you guarantee me that you can sell my

To Receive Your $247 In Free Bonuses: www.TheInsiderSecretsGifts.com

house?" I told her, "There are no guarantees in life. I've sold a bunch of houses and I'm pretty sure I can sell this one." I had no shadow of a doubt that I could get it done, but at the same time, I cannot tell her I will guarantee that. That's not how I do business.

Mark, what I say when they ask me about guarantees...I say, "Did you guarantee the bank that you'd make the payments on this house?" You see, sometimes, even if we have the best of intentions, things don't always go the way we planned. So, the answer is, "No, I can't guarantee it, but I'm confident in my ability to get the job done."

That would definitely put it into a perspective that they understand. So, getting deals is not the problem. Like Paul said, he has an automated system, and he's giving you great suggestions. Go to www.Google.com and type in "sheriff's foreclosures" in your county to see if they're available...and that's just one way.

I've even seen counties that have all of their information in an Excel format on the website. We can do a mail merge right there, and print mailing labels from the site.

This is the thing, though, Paul. All of us know that this is all about abundance. There are so many deals out there that everybody on this call times 100,000 couldn't do all the deals. There's always going to be enough deals...that fact is forgotten all the time.

I think that it's great that you're sharing

175

these different tips and strategies that you use, Paul. It's just so powerful, and there are so many ways...I mean, we could talk about this for hours and days on end about all the different kinds of ways to do deals.

But, I recommend you learn one or two ways...max...stick with it, become an expert in it, and if you want to expand, then you expand. I do my business totally different than Paul, and Paul does his business totally different than many people I know. But it doesn't matter, we're all successful in our own way.

I'll tell you something else...get out and network. Get out to your local clubs, your REIA's (Real Estate Investors Association), and, at the risk of sounding self serving, go to www.WCRT.org if you're in Northern Illinois, Chicago, Southern Wisconsin, etc., get out there and network. I go to the Midwest REIA. I think it's in Elgin or South Elgin at a college campus, but you can look this stuff up...find your nearest REIA and go. There are so many resources that you've got to turn off the TV and get out of the house.

That's how Paul and I actually met is through networking. Right, Paul?

Yes, we met a couple of years ago at one of Frank McKinney's awesome charity events for the Caring House Project Foundation...raising some money for a good cause. Sometimes you'll have to pay to get in to events (but there are also free events out there), but remember that it's an investment in your business' future because there will be people in there that are doing it and making

176

it happen, and you want to surround yourself with those people.

Go to hidden networking places where most people aren't thinking it will do them any good to go to...it's not just at real estate investor network clubs where you will find great people to do business with. At events like Paul's talking about, these are people that are "do-ers". If they weren't do-ers, they wouldn't be investing that kind of money to be at those kinds of things. And these events are so cool too.

Again, you don't want to be a shark either, but if you hear of a job fair that's in town, go check it out. Guess who needs to sell houses? People that are in-between jobs...and those are the folks who will be at the job fairs. Not only that, but the vendors there...a lot of them are entrepreneurs. Make yourself a known resource and presence wherever it makes sense to do so.

I'm known in my church congregation in the west suburbs. The counselors there know who I am and know what I do for a living. People tell them things, and, even though they obviously can't disclose that information to me, they can refer them to me, and have them give me a call. They stay professional yet can give people the tools to help themselves by way of coming to me to see what I can do, if anything.

I may get a call, and I may be able to work something out that they didn't even know was possible. A lot of these sellers have no idea what's possible. They have no idea that the bank will do a forbearance with them. They have no idea that you can do anything like a short sale

177

and get a waiver of deficiency judgment...they just don't know.

It's like anything in life. You don't know what you don't know.

Yeah, be an expert.

Exactly. But, be an expert with just one or two things. I know there's someone reading this that's thinking, "It's just got to stop." Today's the day to say, "Ok, enough is enough."

I can't remember the last time I watched TV, and I actually want to throw in a "plug" for this guy's movie that I just saw. I've been talking about this for awhile now...it's called <u>www.thesecret.tv</u>, and you can watch it online for $4.95. It talks about why 1% of the people make 90% of the income. It is so key, and it's so enlightening to see it and to turn...

I don't want to give the secret away, though, so just check it out. It's so inexpensive but yet it's made one of the biggest impacts on me. I've bought 11 of the DVD's already and am giving them out to the closest people I know. Paul, I don't even know if you're aware of that, but this movie is amazing.

I'll be checking it out tonight.

These are the things. This is what these interviews are for and what I like to call "masterminding". When I was talking to people about doing this interview, some said, "So, hey, you're going to talk about real estate investing... blah, blah, blah." Yes, but *this* is real estate

investing too...the idea isn't to teach you 500 different ways to do deals. If you don't know the "secret" and don't have this one thing down-pat in your mind, I don't care how many ways you know how to do a deal, you're never going to be as successful as you want...guaranteed. You might make it a little bit of money, but true success is a process with continuous growth happening all the time. Get involved with the people that you can help and that can end up helping you...bring value to as many people as you can and it will come back to you 100-fold.

Absolutely.

One of my first big-time mentors that I really stepped up to the plate and invested money with ended up being the best investment I ever made. I took that step ten or so years ago because I wanted to get to the next level, and I knew what I had to do to get there.

I ended up buying a bunch of my mentor's books after that because I wanted to become a person of value to others too so that I could plant the same seeds that were planted with me. I've handed out many, many of them for free to people I've met along the way because he taught me that one thing. I bought at least 1,000 of these books and just hand them out. There's nothing more powerful than handing someone a book and saying, "Here you go. Thank you very much." The first thing out of their mouth is usually, "How much do I owe you for this?" "Nothing," I say, "Read it, implement it and enjoy it." They will remember you forever!

Some of the risk you'll be taking, you mentioned, is spending money with coaches and mentors. I've spent a good deal of money on coaching and mentoring myself in a variety of areas. It can be looked at as a risk to do that. It's stepping out there and putting money on the line. But, you don't have to put a bloody fortune out there right out of the starting gate. What you do have to do is find the right one for you...no one that's hugely successful has gotten there by themselves, I can guarantee you that.

There are resources, but what you do have to do is...I'll just tell you this...you will not make any money on your couch watching television! So, really, turn the thing off. There are some of you who ought to turn it off just for seven days – try and go a week. Just turn it off. During the time that you would ordinarily have it on, do something real estate related.

Go read a book. Go to a website to visit and get information off of it. Take a course. Go to your local REIA or your local entrepreneur's club...some kind of networking. Just get yourself out there and be amongst people because networking is just so key to your success. You're not just looking for property leads...you're also looking for money to do deals with.

Contrary to popular opinion, you *do* need money to invest in real estate...you just don't need your *own* money. But, if you're not going to use your own money, you're going to need institutional financing and/or private investors. You're going to need to find sources of cash. You're going to need contractors. You're going to need real estate agents. A lot of guru types are down on Realtors, but I'm not. A good buyers

180

agent and a good listing agent are two people you want to have on your team.

Yeah, I'm not down on agents or any of those people. I'm only down on the bad ones... they're not all created equal, though.

And, like any other field in life, about 95% of the people don't do very well...about 5% of the people are focused and dedicated. The Realtor you want is the one that's hard to get. I don't mean the one that doesn't return your phone calls because that's all of them. What I mean is that you want the guy that is...if you call him on one of his listings, and he says "I'm busy I'll call you back." You want *that* guy. You don't want the guy that falls all over himself telling you how wonderful this cottage house is, how quaint it is (which means "small" for those of you who aren't familiar with the lingo). You need to find the people in life that are kind of hard to get to. The harder they are to get to, the more likely it is that they've got something going on.

Just to show you a couple of powerful things about networking. Paul and I met over two years ago, and we're really just now starting to build a relationship. We were inner-twined with achieving our goals, but now it's our time to come together and figure out how to do something together.
Keep in mind that it's not a dirty word to make money. A lot of people ask me, "What do I say when I call a seller or buyer? Do you have a script I can follow?" Just say what you're thinking...just be you.

181

Don't be afraid to say you're an investor and that you're going to make money by working with them. Money and profit are not dirty words. I've never lost a deal by telling someone that I'm going to make money. Not only that, but if they don't want you to make money, then don't do the deal anyway because you're not *going* to make money. Move on. It's not a charity, right, Paul?

That's exactly right. You want to help people but there needs to be something in it for you too or you won't be helping anyone out for very long. I feel that the market will basically sort stuff out, and that some of the best things that have been done for the betterment of mankind have been done with a profit motive.

Farmers do not get up at four o'clock in the morning thinking, "Man, we've just got to make sure Paul gets his vegetables today." They don't do it for me...they do it for themselves. They do it because they have a reasonable expectation that they're going to be able to make money and take care of their families. You are no different.

A great example is if you've ever flown on a commercial airline flight, then you know that they tell you that, in the event of cabin depressurization, an oxygen mask will drop down. Now, if you're traveling with a smaller passenger or someone that needs assistance, you are to put your own mask on first and then you assist others...because if you're dead, you can't help anybody.

I know that you mentioned one of your first mentors before. One of his things to say is, "One of the best ways to help the poor is to not be one of them." It's not bad to make money. Profit is not a dirty word. Profit makes the world go 'round.

Unfortunately, there are unscrupulous people out there, and they make the headlines, but the vast majority of people trying to make money are really just trying to do right for themselves and those they care about.

Inevitably, if you make a lot of money, you're going to help a lot of people...it's just inevitable. Bill Gates revolutionized the world. He made $64 billion in the process, but he has changed our lives for the better...your life and mine.

So true, Paul. It really is so neat. When you're not expecting something back immediately, that is when things will start to happen. When I met Paul, I wasn't thinking, "How can I collaborate with this guy to write a book?", mainly just because we're so busy doing what we do. And, Paul, I know that you didn't think that either, but we were just sitting here, and now we're coming together, and now it's starting to happening... let me help you and then you help me. And we're both bringing value.

And this is networking at its finest. Not only that, Paul, but let's talk about the power of the Internet and of having these systems in place you talked about before.

I'm telling you right now...you need to know that without the Internet, we wouldn't be doing this interview right now. That is how we met up again after all that time ago when we first met... that is why you're talking to me now, because of the power of the Internet.

With the Internet, you can get your message across within 5 minutes, 5 hours, 5 days — a lot quicker, smoother and easier. And then you build your rapport with your customers through this

same method over and over and over...just by staying in touch.

Demand for information flow is so huge... it's SO huge. Just staying connected...and I'm not a big tech guy, I'll be the first to admit it. I outsource this stuff because I'm a big believer, though. Mark gave me some really good advice on my newsletter...our email newsletter...that we're going to implement. The reason it hadn't been done yet is because I don't really do it or think about it that much. I'm not a real big, "How do I really optimize my use of the Internet" kind of person, but I've learned from experts that are around me, and today Mark probably gave me a $100,000 piece of advice.

Yeah, and I'm only asking for 25% of his profits...no I'm just joking, Paul. No, but the great thing is that this is just all great fun. Just be yourself. Enjoy it. Honestly, some of the best parts are in the beginning because you're figuring it out, you're developing it, you're doing it, you're creating this for yourself — no one else. Don't let any of the "nay-sayers" tell you "it doesn't work" because I guarantee that Paul and anybody else who's reading this that's doing it *knows* that it works.

Paul, let's give them your website address again. If you are anywhere within a three-hour timeframe or driving range from the Chicago area, you've got to get there. Meet Paul, shake his hand, get to know who he is. Start to know this guy because he's making things happen. When you're around do-ers things will start happening.

To Receive Your $247 In Free Bonuses: www.TheInsiderSecretsGifts.com

Absolutely. Go to our homepage at: www.WCRT.org and sign up for our newsletter.

So you need to go to www.WCRT.org and get on Paul's newsletter mailing list...read it, absorb it and then go out and implement it.
Paul, it's just so exciting to be able to do these types of interviews with people like yourself who are action-takers. That's why you're here, and that's why I'm excited to get to talk to you.

I want to congratulate everybody who's taken the time to read this. One interesting thing that we do in our group is that we have just enough refreshments for about the first 60 or 70 people that come in the door to one of our meetings. If you come late you don't get any. If you come in late, you might not even get to sit down. We do this because you want to emphasize that action-takers are rewarded.

By getting to a meeting just a few minutes early...how hard is that? Just get there five minutes early and be prepared and be focused and paying attention. That's the kind of thing that's going to set you apart. The difference between ordinary and extraordinary is that little word "extra"...it's just going the extra mile. So, we just want to congratulate people that took action and got this book and are going to use it to grow and boost their businesses – and life – immediately.

I also want to say that I can't say enough about Mark Evans...he's just a stand-up guy. He's an investor...he does this stuff every day. A lot of "gurus" haven't done a deal since 1975, and they're still talking about assumable mortgages. One of the things I like about Mark is that his

185

business is different from mine, but his information is fresh. It's relevant. You can apply it today. For those of you that are part of his network, pat yourselves on the backs, stay plugged in and get the information that Mark's got. Get involved and take action!

Thank you, Paul. Once again, go to www.WCRT.org to get involved in online networking and see what events might be coming up that would be good to be at.

Get in there, shake his hand and know who these people are because anybody that's involved in what Paul's doing...they're doing it. Like Paul said, when you send off this vibe, people are going to start coming around you that are do-ers, not just talkers.

The power of association just starts happening and you get rewarded for it...in many different ways, not just financial. The time spent with your family, doing the things you want to do, traveling, etc. I've experienced a lot of that, and continue to do that.

Paul, are there any other closing things you want to talk about or say? I've got to let these guys know how to get these calls because it's not for everybody.

Yeah, I would just say to just keep charging ahead. If you haven't done a deal yet, and you've been kind of kicking tires for awhile, partner with someone on a deal to just get that first one done. If you don't have good credit, partner with somebody that has good credit and some cash.

I don't mean to be flip about it, though. If you think it's easy...well, sometimes it is difficult.

186

People with good credit have worked very hard for that. People with money have worked very hard for it. They'll want to know why they should partner with you.

I'm not going to make it sound easy like some of the "gurus" do, but if you show them that you're serious and dedicated and helpful and will bring some value, like Mark said, then there are people that will help you to get that first deal done. You've got to be willing to show up when you say you'll show up and really focus and work hard. These people that will help you are what I call "Angel Investors". They'll come along side you and help you to get your first deal done.

Don't just *not* do that first deal because of whatever limitations you see ahead of you. If you're really having trouble, contact me via the website and let me know what your stumbling block is. If there's one thing that's really holding you back...if you can just do this one thing then you'd take action and your life would be better and all that, then just shoot me an email and tell me what that one thing is. Let me see if I can help you out or a least point you in the right direction.

I guess what I'm trying to say is "don't stop yourself". If nothing else just read a book, just take action...every day. I know Mark's mentor he talked about before has a question that you should ask yourself everyday, and it is, "What's the one thing that I can do today that I don't want to do, but if I did it, it would move me forward?" I recommend figuring out what that one thing is everyday and start your day by doing it.

Even if it's as simple as, "Taking out the

trash." Even if it's that simple because then you're in motion.

We like to say that 80% of success is just showing up...so, show up! Show up for your success. Get out of your house...get moving!

It's true. Paul, thank you very much for taking this time with me. All of you reading this have really got to get to www.WCRT.org and check this stuff out. It's growing by leaps and bounds. There is no better person to be around than Paul and the people that he's associated with.
We've talked about a lot tonight. Hopefully, you've been taking notes.
Paul, thank you very much...I do appreciate it.

Thank you Mark. I'm glad we got to do this. It was fun.

All right, everyone...go out and start taking action now!

Chapter Six
Interview with Gina Clifford

I have never interviewed anyone that has anything to do with the subject of Short Sales. The reason for that is because I never found anybody that "walked their talk", and those are the only kinds of people I do business with. I think this is a huge problem that faces this industry. Most people don't do what they say they're going to do, right, Gina?

That's true.

This is Gina Clifford from Chicago. We're going to discuss different Short Sale processes, etc. So, have a pen and paper, and be ready to take notes guys because we're definitely going to touch on topics that are taking the nation by storm – and you need to know about them so you can help others too. So, without further adu, Gina, are you on?

I am.

Excellent.

Thanks so much for having me, Mark. I really appreciate it. I'm really excited to be doing this interview for your book because I think it will be read by a group that maybe hasn't heard too much about this subject before.

I love talking to new investors about this

subject. Many people may have heard the words "Short Sale" before, and maybe they know a little bit about foreclosures but many investors have misconceptions of what a Short Sale really is. These kinds of questions always come up:

- How much is a foreclosure?
- How long does it take?
- What exactly is a Short Sale?
- What kinds of offers are good offers to make?
- What are good properties to buy?

Absolutely. Can you give us a quick background on you – a short bio. Can you just explain it, in detail, how you got started in this business before we even dive into the core of the subject?

OK, sure. I'll try to give as much detail as I can. I used to work in Corporate Relocation, most people reading this were probably in the corporate world at some point or maybe still are. My husband and I got married and had a double income with no kids, which is always nice. Shortly thereafter my husband passed his apprenticeship and now as a full time plumber made an extra $5 per hour.

So, with the extra money we had coming in we decided to buy a Corvette. Logical decision, instead of maybe, investing? So, we took our money and bought something that just kept us in the "rat race". After about a year or so, we realized that we were in a position where we were just going to continue making more money and spending more money.

**That's pretty much what always happens...
more money in means more money going back
out.**

Then, my husband came home one day
with a CD called "Rich Dad Poor Dad" that he had
borrowed from his brother. We listened to about
an hour of it during dinner and, when we shut it
off, we literally sat there in silence. Neither one of
us had anything to say because although no one
said it aloud we knew that something had spoken
to us. We thought maybe this was "it", that this
is how we can get out of this rat race situation.
We always knew we were different, destined for
greatness. But How? A couple weeks later, I come
home and there was a package on the kitchen
counter, and it's the Carlton Sheets program. I'm
sure everybody has bought that at some point,
right?

Absolutely, yes.

So, the long and short of it was that we
decided (made a pact) that we were going to
listen to the whole CD set twice before we were
going to look at any properties or make any offers.
Within the first 3 months, we ended up buying a
property.
From that point on, we would buy a house
and do the fix up ourselves. But, instead of just
fixing it up like a regular person would do, we
decided that if we're going to do this we're going
to really *do it* – we were going to be serious. So,
I quit my job. I had a full-time job with a great
salary, company car, company phone...but I quit
it to become a real estate investor.

To Receive Your $247 In Free Bonuses: www.TheInsiderSecretsGifts.com

So, now I was going to help my husband rehab this house. I mean, I was mudding and taping and laying tile – you name it. Which, if you see me, I'm a girly girl, you wouldn't expect it. Then we decided to sell the house that we lived in, sold my car and the corvette and then rehabbed and lived in the next five properties that we bought. We'd buy the property, move into it, and fix it up while we were living there. Then, we'd resell it flip the property into a 1031 exchange and move to the next house.

Then we found the worst house – this was not a house we could live in. It was terrible...crack needles in the walls, mold, rat feces. It was just a terrible, terrible house. So, we had to move into an extended stay hotel instead and lived there for six months.

Oh my. That's what I call dedication, Gina.

From there, Mark, we moved into my parents' basement. Now, I know this all sounds very luxurious I'm sure. But, the point is, if you ever read the book *Think and Grow Rich*, there's this segment about "burning your ships". It's about how, at times of war they went into battle ages ago, they would literally take the ship to the battlefield and then they would turn around and burn their ships so there were no hopes of retreat. Then there was no choice. It was either win the battle or you would die.

There is no turning back, there is no going home...and that's how we looked at it. I had quit my job – I had burned my ship. We were living in the properties. We were going to make this work, and we were committed, we were serious, and it was awesome...and scary all at the same time, you know?

Boy, do I know. I think you touched on a couple of big things I would like to expand on that real quick. Commitment is the first thing. Second, it IS scary because it's the unknown. You think you know where you want to go but, yet, you've never been there, so it is the unknown. This is what a lot of people wait for in this business — for everything to line up exactly right before they ever take action, and it just ruins a lot of peoples' dreams by doing that because I've never heard of things happening like that. It's all about getting the jitters out and taking that first step.

So true. I'm trying to skip past the not-so-exciting part. But, just so people understand the impact this had on me. I took pictures of our "home" when we were living in my parents' basement. The first time I looked at them again was years later, I was teaching a class. I looked at them, and I got choked-up because I looked at them and said, "This is where I lived for a year. That's my bed, that's my desk, and those files on the floor are my office. And there's my closet, which was just my clothes hanging on a rack."

It's amazing to see where we lived, see how we lived — and that's the happiest we've ever been. At that point in our lives, we were so happy because we were doing something that we loved. We were happy, and we felt very fulfilled by it, and that's what's really important. I would rather live uncomfortably for a couple of years so that I can be comfortable for many more in the future. That's how we looked at it.

193

Now, that's how a <u>true</u> entrepreneur thinks, Gina.

That Christmas, we were at a family party, and I found out from my Auntie Harriet that my cousin, Monica, was in foreclosure. She was talking to us because she knew we were investors, and she knew we were purchasing properties and she said, "Gina, you know who has a property you could buy?" It sort of shocked me to think that my cousin was in foreclosure. I knew her story. Her boyfriend that had been living there had moved out. He had no job, and he was selling pieces of furniture in the house for drugs. He even sold the kids' swingset for drugs. This was a very big deal.

We really wanted to be there to help her, and I had just taken a bootcamp on foreclosures, so I thought, "All right I'm going to get out my book, and I'm going to learn how to help my cousin." I called her, went over to her house and called the bank – only to find out that she owed more than the house was worth.

I wasn't sure what I could do to help and the bank said, "Well you can always do something called a Short Sale." So, I said, "What's that?" A bit of back story; by then, my husband and I had probably spent upwards of $60,000 in books and courses and boot camps, but we had never heard the word "Short Sale" because nobody was talking about it a few years ago. That lady at the bank was as sweet as can be and walked me through the entire thing...and that was my very first Short Sale. We didn't get a huge discount – it was a whopping $8,000 discount – and we sold it to a

194

local painter who rehabbed the property.

I say it a lot – that real wealth comes from the small numbers, not the big-number deals.

I agree, Mark. The great thing is that I helped her out of foreclosure, and I was able to get a discount off of what was owed. So, I stepped back and said to myself, "We've lived in houses we've rehabbed. We've done 20 different types of investment deals. We've taken all these classes but this...THIS I have passion for." This stood out to me as I can take something from nothing. I can take something that has no equity at all and negotiate the loan to get it at a lesser cost so that I can actually get a discount. Then she doesn't have to owe anything at the time of closing (my cousin, that is), and I could, at the end of the day, make money off a property that had no equity in it – *and* without having to fix it up.

That was just shocking to me. So I said to myself, "This is something that I've got to keep my eyes open for or maybe I'll never see one of these ever again." But, once your eyes are open to this, you see them everywhere. It's like buying a new car, and you leave the dealership saying, "Oh my gosh, I love this car. Great – nobody has it!" Only to pull out of the dealership and everybody you see has the exact same car. They're everywhere! Foreclosures are just like that. Once you know how to look for them, you'll find that they're everywhere. And that's what spun into my business today performing Short Sales for myself and other investors. I don't talk too much about my history, but I think it's really important for people to understand where I started, where it has taken me, and that you can do it too.

Absolutely, Gina. I think that's excellent. Everything you're saying is so key. It's that subconscious mind — you start seeing things. I was always told you just don't know what you don't know. Once you know it and you realize it, like you said, you see these things everywhere. I don't want to say it's a sickness...but it's so exciting and fun and energetic. So, when we're doing real estate or working on other projects, it's almost like once you find the stuff, you start to see all this abundance of it. It's out there you just don't even know it...even though it's right in front of you right now!

I think it's great to see that and understand that and start taking action on it. That's why I love doing these interviews — it opens people's eyes to the possibilities that are out there and that are available to you...readily available. I mean, there's so much out there. And competition...I don't believe in competition. What do you think about competition, Gina?

I agree with you about not believing in competition. I'll tell you what. Whenever I talk about Short Sales, people raise their hand and say, "Yeah I've heard of it." But, when I ask how many people are doing Short Sales in the room... there's 2 people that raise their hand in a room of 100. So, I'm thinking to myself, "You guys complain about how you're competing against so many people for these properties. Well, look how many people you're competing against right now. There's maybe 2 or 3 people in the room doing this. In Cook County, IL alone there's 300+ foreclosures a week – brand new foreclosures. Imagine how many of those people are upside down, given the state of the economy, and how many properties are over-leveraged, how many people got ARMs or interest-only loans that are now turning into "regular" payments.

It's amazing to think that if there's only 3 of us "competing" for these deals...well, I think we can handle them all. I think there's going to be an abundance left over and you won't have to feel like you just clawed out the eyes of another investor to get the best deal. You can create the equity. So, no, I don't think there's really any competition at all.

No, not at all. And, actually, if done right, you can make these people your partners and leverage each other to make it even bigger and make more money. That's what we've been very good at doing.

Absolutely, Mark.

Gina, can you just explain what a "Short Sale" even is? There are a lot of people that don't know exactly what that terms means. Can you just kind of shine the light on what a Short Sale is?

Of course. In case everyone does not understand about foreclosures. A foreclosure is where someone is behind in their mortgage payments. Usually 3 payments or more and their lender is filing a lawsuit to take back the property. When someone is in foreclosure or behind on

197

their mortgage payments – a Short Sale may be a possibility. A good short sale candidate is when someone owes close to or more than what the house is worth. Plus if you consider a large amount of rehab that can also push a house into a good position for a short sale.

In those cases, we negotiate with the homeowner's lender to have them accept a discount on the amount owed and consider that to be payment in full. This literally wipes the slate clean for the homeowner – they don't have to bring any money to the table at closing, and they're not going to be liable for any discount the bank takes. So a Short Sale is where the bank is going to take a discount on the balance owed, yet consider it to be payment in full.

Some people reading this are probably saying, "Yeah right...banks would never do that." Can you explain the process of something like this ...especially in this day and age. I know every deal is different, but how many banks are willing to do this kind of transaction and how smooth/ quick does it usually go?

I've never had a bank tell me that they're not interested in doing a Short Sale. The thing is that there are many different reasons why a bank *would* want to take a Short Sale – why they would want to take less now rather than carry it through the entire process. Time value of money. One of the biggest reasons is...somebody has to make the payments.

Just because the homeowner isn't making them anymore doesn't mean that nobody has to.

The bank borrowed the money from somewhere too – from the Federal Reserve. So, if the homeowner doesn't make the payments, the bank has to. Believe me, they don't want to make your payments for you – they want to collect the payments, they want to collect the interest. They don't want to own your property, they want to collect your monthly payment. The bank is not interested in owning these properties.

I think a lot of people don't know this...that it's a _bad_ thing for a bank when they have to take a house back. It cuts into their profits and costs them money by having to have attorneys start working on the foreclosure process.

A lot of times, homeowners have come upon a hard situation where something sad has happened in their lives – usually the top three, from what I've seen, are death, divorce and loss of a job. So, many times the house is far below par in repairs. People who are in this situation ...well, the house is usually the last to go. At this point, some people say it's kind of like a sad country song where the girlfriend left, the dog ran away, the truck broke down and then there's the house...and that's the last to go. Usually, these folks still have cable TV, their cell phone and their house, they are scraping to get by and don't have the money to fix the little things, so the house is usually in disrepair.

So, for these different reasons plus much more, is why the bank would be motivated to take a discount today versus waiting until the Sheriff Sale, hopefully, resell it and maybe get the same amount, if not more, later on. They definitely

199

would rather take the discount now. They want to pay off that non performing note and loan that money back out to you and I at 8% or 10% as soon as possible.

Exactly, Gina. As we are moving forward, can you explain to us who your type of business is for and what your lifestyle is like with doing Short Sales? Can you kind of shine the light on the lifestyle you have? Can someone who's sitting at home and has never done a deal in their life...can they understand this easily enough to be able to implement it and take it to the level that you've taken it to?

And, when I say a "short amount of time", I'm not talking get-rich-quick, but I'm talking 2, 3, 4 years of really applying yourself while making money and learning as you grow. Because you're not going to learn it all at the beginning. So, is that possible for someone in the beginning to do?

Absolutely. These types of deals are great for, the first-time-investor or a brand-new investor because, from the beginning, we're normally taught to wholesale everything. Get a property under contract and sell it to the next guy. These properties are great for those types of transactions because the spread is up to you. You build it with your negotiation skills. In a Short Sale, you don't need money out-of-pocket — it's just time and energy.

Yes. Great, what kind of time frame is involved on a typical deal, Gina?

A Short Sale takes anywhere from 3 to 5 months to complete. Initially you are gathering all of the homeowners' financials just like if they were getting the mortgage for the first time. W2's, pay stubs, tax returns, bank statements ...you're gathering all of their financials. They also have to write a letter (called a "hardship letter") explaining why they're in that situation. What happened in their life that they can no longer make the payments? They have to detail everything, from the time everything was going great, life was happy and they were making their payments on time until today...what happened?

The bank's going to review all of that paperwork, and they're going to review the financials and make sure that the hardship letter and the financials match up. So, just saying, "I can't make the payments because I lost my job" but, yet, they collect a monthly income or monthly paycheck (like from government assistance) – that doesn't "add up". The information in the financials has to match up. We add this to our other back up documentation and package it in a Short Sale Package for the lender.

What can take so long is getting the homeowner to gather what they need to gather ...people always procrastinate, even though it's in their best interests to get it done fast.

That is true. Then, the lender is going to order an appraisal, or a Broker Price Opinion (BPO), in order to verify that the offer you're making on the property is a valid offer – and you're going to back that up (your offer) with documentation and repair estimates. If you say that house has problems and needs a new roof or needs new windows, the bank is going to say, "Well, prove it to me. Give me an estimate, show me some pictures." So, you're just doing homework as if you were buying it yourself.

Sometimes I feel like I'm on *CSI*. Doing homework on the house to prove my case. But, it's fun, and you're putting together this package to prove why the homeowners situation is worth a discount and why your offer is a valid one. You're not just low-balling them, you're coming up with a valid offer. This research you can do in your spare time. You don't have to do the homework during the day, you can do that in the evening. You don't have to do it during work hours, and that's what's nice. You can send the package to the bank at night. It doesn't have to be done during business hours – especially if you have a regular job.

I think so many people _do_ think that they have to be able to have daytime hours free to do this business, but they really don't, is that right, Gina?

Yes...a common misconception. I could be working a "regular" job and take a phone call from a bank and say to my boss, "Excuse me, I have to go take a break really fast" and say that I'm taking a smoke break like some people do. Maybe I go on my break to negotiate a property.

Then, at the end of the day, you have a little chess match back and forth with them on the price. If the bank says "OK, well, I think it's worth 160k" and you say "Well, I only want to pay 130k." Then you volley back and forth and negotiate – that's fun. I love it!

If you only have 1 or 2 files going, it's just a few phone calls here and there and little bit of paperwork that you do. You can *absolutely* do this job from start to finish while working a regular career or job.

And that's the people that we have . . . we have a mixture of people in our network. Some that do have a job, some that are looking for a departure from their job, but they just need to find their niche in the real estate world.

One thing I advocate is not trying to find and do 20 different niches. Focus on one, become an expert, understand the fundamentals of that and then go out there and apply it to something else if that's what you want to do. Wouldn't you agree, Gina? That was biggest changing point in my life, anyways...when I became an expert in one niche and stuck with it.

That is so true. And that's why, when I when I went through this with, Monica, my cousin, I realized that, out of all the classes I've taken, out of everything that I've done *this* is it, this is my niche, this is what I want to do.

"It" may not jump out and speak to you. You may try three years of something else before you find the one thing you want to do, but I think you should absolutely choose one thing and go for it. You should know how to do "Subject To" deals and "Lease Options", just in case you come across one of those properties out of the blue, for example. I think you should absolutely choose a niche. Choose a specialty, and give it your all. You can make this happen - you don't need to be jack of all trades.

And a master of none, right? I've seen so many people struggle with this, and I actually did too, when I first began. I tried to do 20 different niches all at once. The problem in real estate investing is there's too many ways to make money, and they all sound good, however, it's dangerous to your success if you don't focus on just one niche.

I do a lot of wholesaling — that's actually most of my business, wholesaling and subject to. The thing is that there may be more per deal money made on the deals that you're doing versus what I'm doing. However, you like that side of the business, and I like this side of the business.

So, Gina, could you give a typical example, if you would, of a profit or how a deal would flow from start to finish and what the profit would be on something like that.

Sure. Let me go over how a deal would flow because I want to make sure everybody understands what a Short Sale is and how it works. I glossed over it before, but first you market to the homeowner and set an appointment to meet with them in person. Let's say you're going to go meet with the homeowner today, you need to gather from them gather all the information the bank needs during that appointment. You might have to help them locate the items sometimes.

So, in a perfect scenario if, you receive all the documents from them that you need today. Tomorrow, you're going to call the bank, and you want to fax in an authorization to release form which gives you the ability to speak to the bank on behalf of the homeowner.

You do have to wait for the lender to get that and put it on file, though, right?

Right. This may take 24-48 hours. Then, you're going to put together your Short Sale package. You're going to ask them, "What time of information do you need, Mr. Banker?" From experience, you'll know they're all looking for the exact same thing: W2's, pay stubs and, tax returns. As if you are applying for a mortgage for the first time.

So, I'm going to put all of this together, and I'm going to place it in a beautiful comb bound package. That's going to impress the heck out them. Then, I'm going to overnight it to the bank. I'm not going to send them a big huge fax because who wants to receive 70 pages in a fax? Not me...and I want my deal to look good. I want the cream to raise the top. I want them to see all those other deals and look at my beautiful package that came in and say, "I'd rather work on that one first."

Legally, the banks have 30-45 days to review the whole package. That's a lot of information for them to review. If everything looks good so far, they're going to order the appraisal or BPO (Broker Price Opinion) and send someone out to place a value on the property. I always go out there to meet them at the house and make sure to point out all the problem areas that there are (so I can justify a lower price later).

The goal is to point out every little ding and leak and everything to get that price knocked down. Correct?

Yes. By the time the bank gets the opinion of the broker back, or the appraisal, it's maybe a week or two weeks later – and that's when the negotiation begins. This phase can last a week or could last two months, depending on how far away you are from each other (in agreeing on the price). If you're $10,000 away that's simple. If you're $70,000 away, that might take quite a few counteroffers back and forth, depending on your skills, which you can absolutely hone in over time.

At that point, when you agree on a price, I always ask for 30 days to close because, like you, I don't like to buy them anymore. I like to wholesale them to the next guy. By the time I'm done with the Short Sale, I'm ready for the next one. I've done a lot of rehabs in my day, and I prefer to just hand it off to the next rehabber.

So, that whole process can span 3-4 months right there. The most fun for me is the negotiating part of the Short Sale. I like to gather everything as if I'm on CSI. I love the negotiating part because it's all about building a rapport. Anybody can do that...you can easily learn that skill. So, that's the Short Sale process from beginning to end. Cliff Notes Version.

You touched on a huge part of this business. Most skip over building that rapport, but it is so key. Also, Gina, what kinds of profits can you expect?

As far as the type of profits you can make, it's unlimited really. It's all on you to decide that. I'll give you an example of one...but please

206

excuse me if my numbers don't add up correctly, as I don't have a calculator here next to me.

I had a property that was here is Elgin, which is where I live. It's about 30 miles west of Chicago. The homeowner owed about $150k. The house was worth, in its current condition, maybe $130k's. After repaired value was about $190k (when fixed up).

The bank had two appraisals and we negotiated for some time. Finally, the bank came down to a price of $106k, which was great. The man at the bank called me and told me, "Gina, that's the lowest I can go, $106k...that's it. I swear on my kids, that's the lowest I can go."

Well, I don't like to take "that's the lowest I can go". I like to always ask for a little inch more. So, I said, "Gosh, I don't know if that's going to work for me. I'm going to have to talk to my partner and get back with you." I hung up the phone and was jumping up and down excited because I knew that was the number I had wanted, but I was still going to ask for more. You never know unless you ask.

Like you said, it's like a chess game, and I love it!

Well, the next day, I called him back and said, "You know, the highest I can go is $97k" and he said, "Alright." So, an extra $9k I got just because I asked for it. So, let's see...they owed $150k, and I got it on a Short Sale for $97k. At the end of the day, the bank netted $87k because I had asked for real estate commissions, and I also asked the bank to pay some of the closing costs for the seller and maybe a little bit for the buyer.

We then wholesaled it to another investor for about $104k. So, $7k for our efforts plus the real estate commission. That investor owned a construction company, so he put a little bit of work into it and rehabbed it — I want to say maybe $25k. Down the road, he resold the property for $198k, which was the top of the market because it was in such great condition. I got a Short Sale of $97k, The bank netted $87k and some change. The investor bought it for $104k and resold it for $198k. I can give you this property address if you want to look it up yourself.

That's an almost $100k difference from what the bank netted to what the end investor walked away with at the end of the day...but, I left money on the table for everybody. The bank was happy because they ended up walking away and receiving something today versus waiting a couple more months until the foreclosure process was over. I was happy because I negotiated a Short Sale and made $7,000. The homeowner's happy because they're out of foreclosure. The end investor is happy because he put $25k into it and made a gross profit of $69k.

There is definitely profit in there. Not every deal has this huge of a spread, though. On some deals, maybe the end guy walks away with $20k or $30k, but I'm ok with that. These are great deals because you can _create_ the spread. That's what I like the most about it is that I have control over creating the spread.

That's excellent. I think that's a huge key. A couple of things here...I see so many great, great investors that are very smart and intelligent,

but they let this little thing inside of them called "greed" get in the way of making them a lot of money.

What happens is that they don't want to leave enough room on the table. They try to squeeze every dime out of it and then, once they do that...well, you might get away with it a couple of times, but the word gets around — especially in the investment market — and people will smack you down for it. Then, you're not going to have an outlet for your deals anymore.

That is so true.

I see it happen all the time. You just want to shake these people and say, "What are you doing? You're so smart." I think what happens is they have the "scarcity mentality". They only want to do a couple deals, so they horde them to themselves, and they max them out every time.

If they would just do it little by little instead, kind of like wholesaling or what you're doing or I'm doing but, doing it consistently...they would reap so much more. Number one, they would make a lot more money in a lot less time and have more fun doing it. Would you agree with that, Gina, from your past experience?

It's so true. Then, you would have a constant buyers list. If you treat them good, they're going to come right back begging for more. They'll be saying, "That was a good one. I want another one, what do you have coming up? I want another property right away." They'll be knocking down your door.

But, if you're trying to make $45k and only

209

leaving $25k for the end guy...it's a small world of investors, and it will come around. Then, all of a sudden, you'll have nobody to sell your deals to because everyone's been warned that you're not the best person to do business with because you've become known as being greedy.

And that's not what you want to do. You touched on this too, and I preach this...having a list, an outlet to sell your properties to is sooo key.
If you don't mind, could you shine the light on how you've built your list over time and give us a couple tips or techniques that we could share with the readers so they can do it themselves too?

Absolutely. Maybe I can get some heads to nod in the audience here because I don't know how many times I've given out my business card to somebody and they said, "Let's get together. I'll call you." And no one ever calls me. Or, let's say you met someone, exchanged business cards, found it two years later and thought, "Who was this person? I kept it for a reason" and then you toss it because you can't remember.

Well, I don't treat it that way. If I meet you, I don't just put your business card in my pocket. I take it out, I talk to you about it, I comment on the card, I write notes on card of who you are and what we talked about and then I ask you what you're looking for. I want to remember. Then literally the next day, send you an email and say, "Hi, it was great to meet you. Here's some information about what I do. What kind of properties are you looking for in case I come

210

across something in your area so that I can send them to you. Do you come across many no equity deals? I'll give you a call."

That's so huge...it's such an important thing that people procrastinate on.

Then, I will contact them with every property I have, even if it's not in their area. Because then they start to say, "Wow, she's got a lot of properties. Maybe I only like Naperville, but you've got a lot in Chicago, so maybe I'll start investing in Chicago. Let me take a look at those things." To build your buyers list, go to investment clubs...a lot of different clubs in local areas and network with people. It's not scary, it's not hard, it's just making friends. It doesn't have to be sales pitches.

Then, take the business cards you get, go home with them and contact them again. So many people get flyers and business cards and do nothing with them. The girls, in my office...they make me laugh. They said, "It's as if they walk up to you and say, 'Hey, can you do me a favor with this business card? Can you throw it away for me?'"

Sometimes it feels like people are saying this because they may have good intentions but will never call you or do anything with it. The point of the business card is so that you have this person's information, and they're saying, "Hey, call me." And they mean it, so I say to them, "I can capture no equity deals for you and I have properties below market to sell." Believe me, they're not going to ignore you.

So, I guess what you're saying, in short, is to become a person of value. Go that extra mile that most people never do. It's such a simple piece of the puzzle. Send an email . . . it's not that hard.

So many people, like you just said, they drop the ball on it. They give you the card, and you just throw it away. If you just go that one tad extra mile, you'll build a list. These people give you a card for a reason, so contact them.

Correct. I'm sure that most investment clubs are all the same – there's a big table at the back of the room with everybody's flyers on it. Everyone's got a house to sell or a product to sell or there are realtors, attorneys and a mortgage company with a new program geared towards investors.

You know what I do? I take one of each flyer, and I contact them too. "Would you like to buy more real estate? Or Do you want help selling more real estate? I can show you how with Short Sales." There's a reason why they have their marketing material out there – they want someone to call them. It's worth it. It's easy...not that hard...there's no 'work' in networking.

This is kind of comical to say now, but since we're talking about this...When I first started, I remember I put marketing out at events like this, and I would never get a call, and I would get so discouraged. So, when someone *would* call me, I would eat it up. I felt like I hit the lottery. I'm like, "Yes, finally someone called me. I must be a genius and a marketer now."

The thing is that, as I was doing that, I started to understand what was happening. Every

212

time I call someone now, I put myself back in that position because I was so excited. They took the initiative — that's the first step to show me that they're somewhat of a do-er.

So, I started sorting my list out *and* my friends. This is one of my favorite parts of the business now, building a list of buyers, sellers, and investors. These people call me first and we just start doing deals with these guys because they're do-ers.

You said the key word, *initiative*. You can not get a reward without some risk. It's not so scary to call someone who handed you their business card. It's not so scary to call someone who's flyer is on the back table screaming, "Please call me — I want your business." Take the risk, take the jump, take the initiative. You'll never get anywhere unless you try. You'll never get it unless you go for it.

That is absolutely so true. I hope you guys are taking notes about a lot of this stuff. Some of the things we say you might have heard before, but maybe it just hasn't hit you yet. It's all about repetition. Hearing this stuff and instilling it in your brain will start triggering your memory as you're doing it.

I'm guilty of this still, once in a blue moon, but not very often anymore. A couple times a year, maybe, I'll get a business card and just totally forget to do something with it. Not only do I write stuff down, but I put where I met them and everything too, Gina. Have you done that?

Yeah, me too.

213

Then I put them in a whole database. For me, I've got to do it within a couple hours after I get home, or it's never getting done. I know that's my problem, but it's getting it and just doing it.

Write this stuff down . . . but don't just write it down, apply it immediately. This is something you can go out and do right now after you get done reading. Go through your business cards because I know there are people there that you haven't contacted. It literally starts the process.

And don't be afraid about calling someone and saying, "Hey I got your card seven months ago. Sorry I haven't gotten a chance to give you call, but I really enjoyed our conversation. In case you don't remember what it was about, maybe we can get a cup of coffee together."

This is no joke — God's honest truth right now. Two days ago, I got a call — and this guy's pretty big. He called me up, and I got a message saying, "Mark I'm so sorry I totally dropped the ball on you." We had talked about two weeks ago, and we were supposed to get together a week after that. He's like "It's my fault." He accepted it and told me that.

Immediately, I'm calling him because, to be honest, I forgot too. But, when he said that, I was like, "Ah ha...this guy accepts full responsibility for dropping the ball." It's all about surrounding yourself around these types of people. When he said that, it actually made me feel more comfortable with him because now he's more real to me.

And you probably had a little more respect for him that he had just came out and said, "Hey, listen...I'm sorry I forgot all about you. It's totally my fault. Please call me back. Let's get together." Right?

Exactly. Like Gina said, don't be afraid to call these people and say that seven months has gone by. They probably don't even know how long has gone by anyways. And you'll rekindle relationships and put them back on the front burner and start producing some results with them.

Start building this list. Start being that person of value and just exploding your business. Just off that one little technique, you can get a lot of buyers for your properties the way Gina is talking about. Gina, sorry about that...we got sidetracked for a second.

That's alright.

This is how our conversations go, if Gina and I were just talking together. The first time we spoke, we were going back and forth about all kinds of stuff. And I think this is so great about the way we do things — it's unscripted, it's real and it just happens in the moment. The reason we can do this in the moment is because we do what we say we're doing. We don't have to have a script and hope we're saying the right things.

With the way the market is going and shifting and all that, can you explain how these people can go out and extract these sellers from the marketplace or...I know you said there's 300 sellers per week in your area, in one little county. Do you know the statistics anywhere else? Is it

215

starting to get better or worse for this business?

I wish I had some of my homework in front of me. There have been programs on the news ...on NBC and CBS, The Morning Show and the Today show – constantly talking about how the market is shifting. They're saying it's getting harder to sell properties. The market is flat, people are even offering cars with their houses for sale, and foreclosures are on the rise.

There was an article on Yahoo pages about bankruptcies rising. I don't know the specific statistics, but I do know that we're at a 57-year high for foreclosures. I also know that we're at an all time high for home ownership, but the problem is that bankruptcies and foreclosures are also at an all time high. It's coming...and it's not a tidal wave, it's a tsunami. It's on it's way, and it's huge.

All the interest-only loans and all the ARMs that were done two and three years ago and all the refinancing...I'm seeing so many folks who hit a dry spell and are going into foreclosure. I heard that there was a 75% increase in foreclosure from last year. I'd have to look up some real-time statistics, but with all the homework I do and all the investment clubs I go to, it's just amazing to see the foreclosures continue to rise. I can't imagine it's only in Illinois...I would image it's everywhere.

The thing is that there's so much going on with the way the economy is, like you said with the ARMs and interest-only loans...I can tell you right now that we don't even have to have the homework – the foreclosure rate IS going up. The

216

reality of the situation is that things are on the rise.

Honestly, I'm so glad we're doing this interview because I think this is the best time right now, more than it has been for a long time, to be in this type of business. Just because you're helping so many great people that are in a bad situation. Once you understand this information...

Well, for example, have you ever been at dinner or somewhere and you hear people talking about the stress of going through this process of foreclosure? You immediately feel like you have to turn around and say something because you know what you have inside of you — your specialized knowledge — and you know that you can help them solve that problem, right?

Right.

It happens all the time for me. It's like it's almost attracted to me. I think that's what is so great about this because these people, like you said, are usually facing one of the three biggest challenges — job loss, death and what else?

Divorce.

Divorce. These are all tough situations in and of themselves...then, everything else that just snowballs behind it.

True, many people out there just want to make money, and I want to make money too. I want to be comfortable and happy in my future and be able to support my family, and I want to enjoy myself. However, you need to be a good

217

person too – you *have* to have a good heart.

There are investors out there that are trying to scam homeowners by making the homeowner pay them to do a Short Sale. You could take full advantage of people in this situation. But you can <u>also</u> be their savior. I've had homeowners hug me and bake me pies and buy me pictures for my office, and say things like, "Bring over your husband and daughter for dinner tonight." I had one person buy me a gift when I had a my daughter.

These people love you because you were the only one who said "yes". Every other "We Buy Houses" guy, "Any Price, Any Area, Any Condition" said "no" because they had no equity. But I said, "No equity? No problem. Let me try and help you. There's something I can do. I specialize in this. Here's my track record. Here's my team. Here's everybody that can help you. I know I can help."

Then, at the end of the day, they love you for it. That's worth it's weight in gold. I help them out of foreclosure, feel good about it and I made a little bit of money in the process, that's not so bad.

Exactly. That's the business we're in, is making money.

Right.

While we're talking about this, I know you're associated with Frank McKinney's charity just like we are. We contribute to his Caring House Foundation. You want to talk about that real quick because, you know, it's not just make, make, make and keep, keep, keep, right?

218

That's so true. Frank McKinney's charity is something I support. My husband and I have been donating there since the beginning of 2004 ...since we first met Frank. They build houses for the homeless in Haiti, which is the world's poorest area. In fact, they just got hit by another hurricane.

These homes that he builds are concrete structures that cost $4,000 – and that's it. What we do at my company, Stone Castle Realty/Short Sale Systems and my husbands company Stone Castle Properties, is we donate money from the proceeds of every closing we have to the Caring House Foundation. We're able to save up enough money each year to buy a couple homes for the homeless. After every single closing, we send a letter to the seller and buyer saying that we made a donation in their name to the Caring House Foundation.

It's just such an amazing foundation...I've seen videos and tapes of those areas. To see what someone lived in and their sadness compared the next picture of a cute little bungalow that is painted bright pink with a smiling happy family out front that's going to live there now. It leaves an impact. You've got to give back – then you'll get more in the future. You can't keep, keep, keep, you've *got* to give back.

Exactly. So, you said you started around 2004. I know when I started donating – even when I thought I had no money to donate. Actually, that's when you need to do it the most. I saw an immediate change within 30 days. Now, I'm not saying that it will happen for everybody, but

in my life, personally, I saw a huge shift happen for whatever reason because I committed that money.

I can't say I wasn't scared and shaking when I wrote that check — and it was only a $200 check, I think, the first time I ever donated. I was scared because I probably only had $300 in the bank at the time. But, when I did that, things just started changing immediately, and things almost started happening with ease.

You definitely have to give back. Like she said, it's not always make, make, make, keep, keep, keep. It's make, keep, give, make, keep, give. It comes around full-circle 10 fold, no...I think it's 100 fold.

Not only that Mark, but you feel so good when you're giving and you know where it's going. It's not like it's just going to Frank. You never know sometimes with charities and everything that they do.

We saw Frank again last January. We got rode on his motor home for a leg of his book tour, and he showed us a video of the families and the conditions they were living in. We came back, and my husband Joe said, "We need to donate another house."

He took money from his savings, and I took money from my savings, and we scrounged, and I said, "I have to pay taxes right now. I don't have money for this. Payroll is coming up." But, he said, "Just do it. You've got to do it. It will be good." I felt wonderful afterwards. It's one of those things that you're kind of manifesting. You manifest your destiny, so to speak. So, put it out to the world, and it will come back to you. It will...

220

it will.

You better believe it will. So, I want to touch on this too, Gina, if you don't mind. We've talked about the process, what it takes, etc. to get started in this. Can you show or explain where these sellers are? Just give us a quick glimpse, a 3-5 minute glimpse, of where to find these sellers or how to get them coming to you — as well as your buyers. What kind of strategies do you use?

Seller strategies I use? I always make sure I have multi-marketing going on, different things at one time. Business cards at the gas station, signs in the window, magnets on my car, flyers being passed around everywhere, networking with Realtors.

I purchased a foreclosure database, and I market to and send out mailers too. I alternate mailers with postcards. I write out the letters that I've created that are mailings now, but they're real letters. They're real things that say, "Hey, listen, I've been there. I had my identity stolen. I had to file bankruptcy because two people stole my name and my social security number. I was at a point where I couldn't make my bills. So, I understand where you are. I've been there, and if you need help, call me."

People will call. If anybody else answers the phone they say, "No I want to talk to Gina" because they feel this personal connection to me, and it's true. I believe in telling it like it is — be truthful. That's the best way to approach people. They can read thru any other types of marketing. I don't say, "Hey, you're in foreclosure. Your only way out is to sell it to me." Some people try

221

different tactics – they try to be mean, they try the bank approach, they try different approaches...I just try "real". Here's me, here's my life, here's my company, here's my background, here's some testimonials, call me, and I can help you. When anyone else says 'no' I can say 'yes.'" I know I will help them, and that makes the phone ring. Never underestimate the power of the business card. Give it to everybody. I give it to waitresses and waiters. I give it to the guy at the cleaners. I give it to everybody. On the back, it tells what kinds of houses I'm looking for – foreclosures and motivated sellers – and that I'll pay you a referral fee if you find me a house. It works.

It's so key. She's talking about multi-media, about constantly putting it out there – not doing it once and quitting because you might not get a response. But putting it out there on a daily, consistent basis – that is the key because it starts snowballing. Actually, it becomes a habit if you do it for 30 days straight.
Like she said, she hands them to waitresses, servers, etc. We do that all the time just because it's a habit now. It's like crossing the street, you look both ways because it's a habit. Same thing with handing business cards out, putting flyers out, talking to people or overhearing people's conversations about real estate. It's just a habit that you create inside of you, and it's just crazy. It's exciting to help these people.

So many people get nervous. I think people get that, you know, analysis paralysis. I think people get stuck in this "I don't want to door knock. I'm not that kind of person" or "I

222

don't want to network, it's scary. I'm kind of shy" or whatever the case is.

I look at it as I have something amazing to give. They want it – they just don't know it yet. You have to believe that you have some amazing gift. You have the ability to help them out of foreclosure. When everyone else said, "Nope, I can't help you" you can pull them out of that. You can help them take no equity and build it into equity. I know I can help you, and I'm not shy. I can knock on your door when you call me for an appointment because I know that I have something you want. I know I can help you, and I know that you're going to benefit from that so I'm not nervous about that at all. As my husband says, "Fear is False Evidence Appearing Real"

Look, when you believe that you can – you can. When you believe you can't – you can't. That's the biggest thing for me.

It is so key. The best part of doing that is surrounding yourself with the right people and not trying to re-invent the wheel. By finding people that are doing it daily and then applying their techniques and strategies, networking with them, and just being around like-minded people . . . that will help you to have that "I can do" mentality. So, we talked about sellers, now your buyers. I'm assuming it's almost the same strategy. Correct?

Yes. Another way to find buyers is by networking. Every single investment club you can go to, even if it's two hours away...go. Bring a flyer and bring your business cards. Grab everybody's business card that you can get, like it's a game. That's how you get your buyers. The buyers are easy, but I think a lot of people don't understand that. If you have the good deals, the buyers will come – the money will follow. It's easy to find the buyers…you just need to keep your eyes open for them.

Not only that – because I've been here …I'm talking out of experience when I tell you that when I first started doing wholesaling, I understood that there were buyers out there, but I was so darn broke. I used to do stuff in the hood. We were doing houses at $20,000 to $30,000. Well, I didn't have $20,000 or $30,000 so I put these people in my position. I was like, "I'm too broke to afford it, so how can anybody else?"

You've got to separate yourself from that because I'll tell you right now that $30,000, $100,000, $200,000 really is not that much money compared to what some people have sitting around and are doing nothing with it. I just separated myself it and looked at it in a different way.

I mean, look at Trump - he has more than $30,000, right? Sounds silly, huh? But, that's what I started doing. I started picturing that person buying my property. I knew that he wasn't going to do it – someone of that stature or someone that had that kind of money. That's when the light clicked on for me. My mind just started opening up to a whole different horizon of buyers. There is a lot of money out there.

Could you talk a little bit about what you have going on over there, Gina? I know you have a class that you do, and I know that you have a lot of different materials that you have out there. Can you talk a little bit about that?

224

Yes. Currently, I own a Real Estate Office ...it's about 10% traditional real estate and 90% investment real estate. I have a Short Sale side, Short Sale Systems, and our focus is on foreclosures and Short Sales. I have a large group of people that that's all we do every day. I teach classes to investors and Realtors and to people in all the different areas in Illinois about Short Sales. I've created an amazing system that works for me and brings in leads and closes deals when I'm not there.

I've been able to take that system that I created in mom and dad's basement, put it on paper and put it into a format that's easy. I've created forms from scratch because, when I first started, there were no forms – there were no gurus available talking about this subject. If there was, I would have snatched it all up. But, I created it all from scratch, and I've created it into a system – a short sale system that is very analytical and task oriented. I have many "cookie cutter" processes and checklists, it is systemized in a way that's easy for someone else to take and match and turn it into their own.

I have a manual that is step-by-step, and I have a DVD of a full-day class that you can follow along with in the manual. I have a couple different sets of forms – from basic all the way to "TKO", which is "Total Knock Out", which includes everything from building rapport with the homeowner and getting them on your team, all the way through to all the negotiating and power and everything you need to have when working with the bank.

That will totally take the fear out...people are so afraid to negotiate with banks.

I am currently working on a two day class that is more advanced and will feature a real live loss mitigator from the bank. I have a lot of other helpful programs for all levels of investor. There is a project I am working on currently that will blow all the others away and that is the Short Sale Tutor Program. It's a internet based program that teaches you Short Sales as though you have a mentor sitting next to you the whole time. I can't wait! I also have a Staging CD-ROM and pamphlet on how to stage properties if you're going to wholesale them. I have a "Take to the house tool kit" that features picture-taking, and the proper way to take the right kind of pictures for the bank. That's an art in itself, and I've discounted $26,000 from one deal from just the pictures I submitted to the lender. In the CD-ROM is instructions and examples of good pictures and bad pictures plus things to take with you to the house. Like I said, I'm a CSI. I bring my ruler, I bring a tape measure, I've got the gloves and the mask and the whole thing.

I also have a pamphlet of a presentation I did at a ladies networking group about taking the 'work' out of networking, because it's so important that you network constantly. As you can see, I could talk about this for hours.

I'll tell you right now, a three page pamphlet may not sound like a lot, but I will tell you this...if all it would take is one page to cure cancer, how much is that *one* piece of paper worth? I think people confuse a lot of stuff with not much value.

226

Me, being only high school educated, I need things to be simplistic. If I remember right, I saw that you said something in your bio that you've had just with your system 52 deals going on at the same exact time.

By myself and in my parent's basement, I did 52 Short Sales by myself simultaneously.

It's insane. Obviously you have to have something going on because, if not...unless you're balding like me, and I know you're not...you have to have something in place to make that happen and not go nuts. I will tell you right now, like I said, I have searched high and low to find someone of this caliber that can take you to the level you want to achieve because I know this is a huge need and a huge niche that I don't even touch because, quite honestly, I don't get involved in it because it's not my niche. So, my goal and my drive and determination is to find people that can help you get to that level...and her name is Gina Clifford.

Gina, do you have any other things you would like to say before we wrap this up?

I just say take action. If it's something that you want to do, do it. Don't regret it later. Make something out of it. This is an amazing niche. This is a niche that nobody is touching. This is an amazing time, and the tsunami is coming. You're going to see so many foreclosures and so many more Short Sale opportunities. If you're not taking advantage of them, your neighbor is going to. So, take advantage of it.

Not only that, but if you're doing this, and you're putting deals together with Gina's system, and they make sense for investors to buy...I have a huge investor database that I'm willing to let you leverage. I'll allow you to place your deals, if they make sense, on my website for sale to my investors. I have to check them out first, of course, but I have been known to sell properties in minutes, so it will be a huge asset to you to have access to.

That's awesome! I don't think people understand just how great that is – that you just offered that. One of the hardest parts is finding the database. So, you're offering to help them put the property on your database – that's amazing! Folks, you need to take advantage of that.

The thing is, we're here to help. These investors are wanting to buy. I can't supply thousands of people with properties everyday by myself. Go out and get some deals, and let's make money together. I'm all for it, and I know Gina would be nothing more than happy to see her system in motion helping people succeed.

I would love it.

Gina, can you give them us your website address for people to go to so they can read more about your system and sign up for your newsletter?

Of course Mark, they can go to: www.thequeenofshortsales.com and/or www.shortsaletutor.com.

Thank you, Gina, very much for taking the time out to do this interview with me. For our readers, get over to www.thequeenofshortsales.com and/or www.shortsaletutor.com and soak up every word Gina says. She truly is a person that walks her talk and that you need to be hooked up with.

Thank you so much. I had a lot of fun.

Me too, Gina. I wish you continued success.

"The starting point of all achievement is desire. Keep this constantly in mind.   Weak desires bring weak results, just as a small amount of fire makes a small about of heat."

- Napoleon Hill; Author

"I think there is something, more important than believing: Action! The world is full of dreamers, there aren't enough who will move ahead and begin to take concrete steps to actualize their vision."

- W. Clement Stone

Chapter Seven
Interview with Michael Gerber

This is going to be such a great read for you. Michael Gerber has helped me and thousands of other people understand how implementing "systems" will allow you to live the life of your dreams. His principles have worked for me, both in business and in my personal life, and I know they will for you too. So, let's get started...

If anyone can be called "The World's #1 Small Business Guru", it would be Michael Gerber. His e-books have sold millions of copies worldwide. His company, E-Myth Worldwide, which he founded in 1977, has coached and trained over 50,000 small business clients in 145 countries. His new venture "The Dreaming Room" is about to take Michael's entrepreneur insight and wisdom to many millions of people who want to start their own business but don't know how. Michael...welcome.

I'm here! Thank you for having me, Mark.

Michael, I'm so excited to talk to you today, but we only have an hour. So, if you don't mind, let's just jump right into it. What is the "E-Myth"?

Sure. The "E-Myth" is the "entrepreneurial myth", Mark. We work with small business owners who have started companies in over 145 countries around the world. The "E-Myth" essentially says that the vast majority of people who go into business anywhere in the world are not the entrepreneurs that everybody thinks they are.

Instead, they are what I call "technicians suffering from an entrepreneurial seizure". It is people with a particular skill – it might be a sales skill, it might be a cooking skill, auto mechanics, or software guys, cardiologist, attorneys, accountants. In other words, they know how to do something. They are working for somebody, and it drives them crazy. They want to go out on their own. And, of course, in our country it is called going out on your own and creating your own business. "I want to open a business of my own. I want to become my own boss."

It's not always all it's cracked up to be, that's for sure.

Essentially, what drives most small business owners is that desire to "be my own boss", so that's why they do it. Well, the minute they do that, they discover that they made a terrible, terrible mistake. Now they the work that they are good at, along with the other work that they are just absolutely terrible at doing that everybody who starts a business needs to do – the marketing, the sales, the administration, the production, the cleaning up after.

Now, it's getting the money to work, it's getting the people to work, the product to work, the service to work. That calls for significantly greater understanding, skill and experience than 99% of all people that start their own business have. So, as a result, what they do is keep their business very, very small or not at all, and that's

232

the "E-Myth". That's why most small businesses don't work. The book tells you what to do about it.

I've read your "E-Myth" book, Michael, about 20 times. I've read this thing, and I've dog-eared and highlighted parts of it. I've also handed out probably 40-50 books or more. I'm constantly handing it out to so-called entrepreneurs that think they are owning their own business. You talk about something in there that says that a lot of people who work for themselves call themselves a lunatic. Can you expand on that a little bit?

Most small business owners really are working for a lunatic – themselves. They are doing what I call it doing it, doing it, doing it, busy, busy, busy. They got rid of a job working for somebody else and now they've created a "job" by working for themselves, and they are absolutely out of their minds. They are completely controlled by all of these activities that they really don't know how to do. So effectively, something has got to change, and that's really what the "E-Myth" talks about.

Instead of going to work "in" your business, go to work "on" it. When you go to work "on" your business, you begin to understand something completely foreign to the vast majority of the people who own their own business. If your business depends upon you, if the work you do drives your business, then it isn't really a business ...it's a job, and it's the worst job in the world because you're working for a lunatic!

I want to make you sane. I'm not a psychologist, but I want to make you sane. I

233

want to create a way for every single person who owns and operates his or her own business, no matter what kind of business it is – high-tech, low-tech, no-tech, real estate business, software business, a restaurant – to have the one single key that will enable you to transform the reality of that company into a company that works for you rather than because of you.

Then, you'd be suddenly free to do stuff that you would have never imagined that you would be free to do. Most people will never, ever experience being free to do what they want to do ...and that is to really create a life that you can do whatever it is you wish to do, just like I'm doing right now, just like you're doing right now. We live very unusual lives.

It's funny you saying that because I was talking it over with Deena, my fiancée. We were talking about how it is hard to relate to some people because, when I'm talking to some people, like my brother-in-law, he says he owns his own business, but he never sleeps, and he never sees my sister, and he's so stressed out all of the time. I look at his situation because I see myself in him when I first started – he just doesn't get it yet. I've given him the "E-Myth" to read three times, but he still hasn't even opened up the book yet!

While we're talking about this subject, what is the percentage of businesses that fail because of this symptom of working _in_ your business and not _on_ it?

The Department of Commerce and Small Business Administration has information on this for every industry. Depending on who you talk

234

to, roughly between 70% to 90% of all new businesses will fold before they ever reach their 10th anniversary – most of them in their first five years. So, just think about the vast majority of people who take the leap to go into their own business. The other truth is that the vast majority of people who go into business on their own, if they don't outright fail, they absolutely fail to fulfill the potential of that business. In other words, they've got a 12-cylinder engine, but they are only using 1 cylinder.

That's the truth of most businesses. They are just puttering along – not really growing, not really excited, not really creating the income and the revenue and the profit they should be able to create, not really giving the person who owns it the real satisfaction of creating something that is world-class and has truly remarkable capabilities. Most small business owners will never, ever have that experience, and they justify it with, "Well, that's the way business is," and it isn't that way at all.

I suffered through being a "serial entrepreneur" for awhile until I figured out what I wanted to do, and I went through the process. Once I discovered real estate investing, I just knew that is what I wanted to do forever because I have a huge passion and drive for this.

I read the *E-Myth Contractor* because I had a contracting business, and I was working "in" the business every day. After reading that, I said to myself, "I'm going to work "on" my business," and I committed myself to do that. I find that it's scary for some people because I was scared to death. I felt like I was giving up control of what I

was creating.

Oh yes. Understand, though, that the person that is petrified of giving up control is not the entrepreneur. The entrepreneur inside of you, Mark, and inside of me and inside of every single person on the face of the earth is the creator.

The entrepreneur is the inventor. The entrepreneur is constantly asking, "What is missing in this picture?" They are looking around them and constantly seeing that something is "off", something is wrong, something isn't working the way it could work. They suddenly begin to dream about what would make it right. They begin to imagine the possibility of, "How will I do that differently?" They are constantly wondering "how" and "what if" and are constantly in that wondering space. So they don't have time to be afraid of losing control.

That is so very true!

The person who is fearful of losing control is the technician doing it, doing it, doing it, busy, busy, busy, who is *always* feeling out of control, always feeling that something is going to happen to him or her. The true power is in their ability to do it, but, unfortunately, they don't control all of the elements that need to be controlled in order to do it. They are terrified of giving that away to somebody else because they haven't developed the ability to manage it well.

There are three real laws that I talk about in the "E-Myth" – the entrepreneur, the manager and the technician. The entrepreneur is the dreamer. The entrepreneur is the creator. The

236

entrepreneur's vision is of business that works without him, not because of him.

That's the key to true success right there. You have to be able to leave for a week and the business still continue to produce even though you're not there.

Absolutely. The manager is the inventor of the system that enables the business to produce the results that the entrepreneur envisions. The manager does the invention, quantification and orchestration. The manager invents the system through which the entrepreneur's vision is manifested at the operating level of the business.

The technician is the producer. So, the entrepreneur is the inventor, the manager is the enabler, and the technician is the producer. The producer only sees so much, and that is the job that he's got to do – he's caught up in the work.

The manager is caught up in creating a way of organizing the work – to work more productively, more consistently. The entrepreneur is inventing the work that needs to be done in such a way as to produce a result that the world has never seen before.

So, in a very organic way, these three roles are ones that each of us need to develop. I need to develop the entrepreneur in me. I need to develop the manager in me. I need to reduce the impact of the producer in me. Doing this will create more life, more opportunity, more growth... more of everything else around me.

Exactly, and when you really start focusing

on those three things that you need, you will see a change. I never even realized those three things existed until I read your book. I bet most people don't know that either. Once you read The *E-Myth* and you realize you're being those things, it will change everything.

I was being the technician, and it was eating at me every day because I knew this was not the way of the business. Now, I'm in a different state for the last nine months, and we are buying properties all over the country. All I am doing is creating it and having people manage it and be the technicians. When I started doing that, I almost starting feeling guilty.

Now think about that. When you found that you could get the work done through other people, you began to feel guilty. Well, who should feel guilty? The technician, who says, "Heck, I should be doing this. I should be doing this work," and you begin to feel guilty because you feel you're not doing what you should be doing. I hear that from every single client that we've ever worked with over the years.

Understand another very important point is that E-Myth Worldwide is a company that coaches small business owners, but I stopped coaching small business owners in 1979 – two years after I started my company. I started my company to transform small businesses worldwide by developing an intelligent system through which that coaching could be done by other people, not me. And so our company is a product of *The E-Myth*.

In other words, I built the company to produce something I didn't want to do. I wanted

238

to see the results, but the company produces it, I don't. And you do exactly the same thing. The technician isn't the person who succeeds at creating great wealth or expects to produce extraordinary results, the entrepreneur is.

Absolutely. Once I realized that, I found myself becoming more creative and more clear. I had a much more focused action plan for my days too – I wasn't so scattered. I found that I was getting things done without me physically doing them. As it happened, they just started falling into place.

For me, I always felt like no one was going to do it like I could do it – I guess that was the technician in me. After I got an understanding of that and put it into my system, I "got" it. I just kept using it and working it, and things started getting better and better.

You know, you talk about real estate investing. Real estate investors are not business people – they are not entrepreneurs. They don't really invent a business to do this; they create a job for themselves.

They go out and they look for property, they buy it, they take care of it. They are constantly caught up in just about every single thing you can imagine that needs to be done. Do you find that to be true?

Absolutely, that is the one single truth I know, and it is also the thing that keeps me up at night. I'm always trying to figure out how I can make it easier, how I can make it better.

I spend most of my time on creativity. I

probably only spend 20-30 minutes a day, if that, really working "in" it. And, if I'm working "in" it, I'm making money.

But understanding that is a different story. People go out, they get a couple of houses and they think that they are going to be rich and will never need to do anything else. But there are a lot of pieces to the process to get to that wealth that they want to achieve.

Yes, and that has to be done. The entrepreneur sees the opportunity – "if I could get that stuff done without me having to do it myself..." However, he needs to be absolutely certain that it is getting done in a world-class way. If I can do that through ordinary people *and* through extraordinary people at the lowest possible cost but at the greatest possible productivity, then that's what I'll do.

You need to realize that you can do this bigger, bigger and bigger, and then you'd be creating an enterprise, not a business. I could create a company that has an enormous size capability... like a Federal Express, or a McDonalds, you name it. Nobody in real estate investing actually sees that opportunity the way an entrepreneur does – they always fall short of it. The vast majority can never imagine the possibilities. I'm saying a lot of people can achieve that once they understand how to.

And I would venture to guess that at least 99% of people don't understand it.

That's without a doubt.

They're looking at houses, they're rehabbing houses, they're fixing them up, they're talking to tenants, etc. They're dealing with all the issues that come with property ownership, instead of handing it over to other people to take care of.

Sometimes they think it costs money to do that, but I see it so much differently than that. Their time is worth money. If you really figure out the time against the money they are making or receiving, it's less than people make working at McDonalds.

Yep, and it's tragic. And you just sit there and say, "Why in the world can't they see this? It's so clear."

It's almost like you're talking a foreign language to them. Michael, you started this in 1977. Wouldn't you say that it's a lot easier to do all of this now, especially with the Internet? I mean, the *world* is at our fingertips every day.

It gets easier and easier and easier every day, Mark. But the reality is that, until people change, it doesn't matter how easy it is. The same thing is true about the people I talk to today as it was with the people I talked to in 1977 when I started my company. They absolutely don't understand the difference between the role of the entrepreneur, the role of the manager, and the role of the technician. They absolutely don't understand how liberating it can be to shift your attention from one role to the other – from the management role to the entrepreneurial role to truly begin the business all over again but in a completely, new, refreshed and exhilarating way.

I'm saying to you now that anybody can do that. And *that* is where my focus has been for the last 30 years. We have been fortunate enough to literally transform the lives of millions of people. The minute they "get" it, like you yourself have gotten it, is just the greatest moment.

Before we started this interview, you asked me how the weather was in California. I told you it's beautiful here and that the winds were picking up a little...

Then I asked where you were, and you said you were in Maine. You described to me where you happened to be at the moment. I asked if that's where you live, and you said, "No. I don't live anywhere anymore. I live where I show up, and I show up wherever it might be that I'm called to go to." That's just extraordinary. For the past 9 months, I think you said, you have just been traveling.

Yes, and it's a totally different mindset and exactly what I needed. I remember sitting in my office (I had a three-room office) reading *The E-Myth*. I was discouraged, and I was down. I just sat there and kept saying to myself that I knew there had to be something better out there. Everything you said, like, "Well, that's just the way business is run," and this and that...it had all seemed true, but yet I see things differently today.

You walk into McDonalds, for instance. Ray Croc is not in there pushing buttons, so you know there has got to be an easier way. With the power of questions, I came across *The E-Myth*. I don't even remember how that happened, but I came across it, and I remember sitting there reading it

To Receive Your $247 In Free Bonuses: www.TheInsiderSecretsGifts.com

and feeling like somebody hit me in the head with a Louisville Slugger and said, "Mark, wake up!" From that time on, I've never been the same.

You know, Mark, there are probably hundreds of people reading this right now, and they're saying, "What's the gimmick? I mean, come on, what's the gimmick?" The fact of the matter is that there have been millions upon millions of people who have read *The E-Myth* and then *The E-Myth Revisited* and *The E-Myth Manager* and my latest book *The E-Myth Mastery* or *The E-Myth Contractor* or *The E-Myth Physician, Why Most Medical Practices Don't Work And What To Do About It*.

Just put this into the context of real estate investing. The vast majority of people who are reading this now don't trust what you're saying or what I'm saying. They absolutely don't trust it, and they don't realize that their life, right at this very moment, could be exponentially different than what they have experienced since the day they were born.

And, once they do "get" it, they'll kick themselves for not getting it sooner.

To all those people, let me just say that there is no gimmick to this. You can change the way you think about everything. The moment you do that and see the way the world works, the way business works, the way real estate works and the way relationships work...the minute you change your perspective on all of that, everything you do from that moment forward will be absolutely different, and every result that you get will be

243

exponentially different.

This is what our clients and the people who have read my books have experienced over the years. It's like, "Wow, I never realized that. How come nobody told me that before?" All the time, I hear people saying, "My god, Michael, where have you been all my life? I wish somebody had told me that." The minute they "get" it, they say, "Well, of course. That makes sense!"

And it really does make perfect sense when you stop and think about it.

Here's a simple story. Ray Croc was 52 years old when he discovered McDonalds. Now, you have to understand that Ray Croc at 52 was a peddler of malted milk machines, and he had gone to the McDonald brothers in San Bernardino, California to sell them a malted milk machine. The McDonald brothers actually created McDonalds – Ray Croc just discovered it when he went in to sell them the malted milk machine. So, Ray walked into McDonalds with one product, but he walked out of McDonalds with a hamburger stand in San Bernardino, California and a completely different product. The McDonald brothers gave Ray Croc the franchise right then and there.

He went back to Des Plaines, Illinois to start his first store. He borrowed the money to do it, but he had a vision, and the vision was, "I can create 30,000 of these little stores throughout the world – a multi-billion dollar empire – by simply replicating this turnkey operating system that is McDonalds." But, first he said, "I've got to make sure it's absolutely perfect."

But it doesn't even have to be perfect...and it won't be...you'll always be tweaking it to make it better.

You're right. So, when Ray Croc started his first store, he didn't go to work "in" the store. He didn't make the hamburgers or the French fries. He didn't make the malts. He went to work "on" the store, *outside* of the store to get the little sucker right.

The model that he had in his mind was, "I'm going to build the most successful small business in the world. And the most successful small business in the world will have, at its core, an operating system that can be put into hands of ordinary people and kids at minimum wage with 300% annual personnel turnover. I can do that, and, in the process of doing that, I will then have the "DNA" that can be replicated thousands upon thousands of times over and over again and become the most extraordinary business you've ever seen,"...and that's what he did.

That's essentially what I'm saying that every single real estate investor can do, and that's what you have done, Mark. You've built your "McDonalds", a turnkey system that anybody can actually use to build an enterprise.

Absolutely. Michael, what you said that's been so key for me in doing this and going through the process, was that I had to create what I wanted, mentally, and put it on paper to have that vision. By doing that, my mind starting shifting and putting things in place.

Maybe this is how I discovered "The E-Myth" and all these other pieces is through that

process of creativity and what I call "creating my ideal life". I wrote down exactly what I wanted and when I was going to have it...and it almost happened at the exact date I'd written down. I felt like I was too busy to do it, to take the time out to do it – a day or two days or however many days it may take you. But to sit down and write it all out, and just dive into it...to picture yourself there where you want to be or how you want your business run was a huge, monumental stepping stone for me and helped me get to that point.

Yes, it is monumental. Until somebody really "gets" it, they cannot appreciate how monumental it is – it's bigger than life. It's like owning a hamburger stand and going in every day and making hamburgers. Or, conversely, owning a hamburger stand and every day having a manager and workers in the stand while you stand outside and look in on how it all works while you just watch. You've got a bird's eye view of it and can just sit back and watch.

You'll watch the manager manage, and you'll watch the workers make the hamburgers, you'll watch everyone doing this for you – for your company – and you will then begin to see it from above. You now have a planned view of it, and you'll see it all and think, "Wow. Wouldn't it be better if he were to do this that way or she were to do that differently."

So, you go in, and you have a meeting every day, and you describe what you saw and how it can be improved, and they say, "Wow... that does sound better" or "What if we did it this way instead." Then, as you begin to do that, the systems will unfold better and better and better

246

and the company can then expand its capabilities to produce better results. All this, and you're not doing any of it...that's what is so amazing.

And, you know what's amazing? I try to explain this to people, but they really just don't understand, like you said. I guess it seems too good to be true.

Right, but there you are! And they'll look at you and say, "Yeah, but what's he doing? What's the secret behind this? What's he trying to sell me? What's he trying to say?" and so on and so forth when you know that the truth of the matter is that all you need to do is tell the story. You say, "Listen, I learned how to do something, and I'll teach it to you if you're interested in growing." That's all you can do.

Absolutely, and that is the key. Yesterday we were walking around, and it was so beautiful out. Being able to do that is so much better than to be strapped down by something. We were walking by the harbor and, all of a sudden, I got a call from my assistant saying, "Hey, we just sold two properties."

I have never even seen these properties...I have no idea where they're located. I don't know any of those integral pieces of it, but I know we're going to make money. I know our investors are going to make money, and I know everybody wins.

It was all done systematically, where my assistant only spent probably 20-30 minutes on the whole transaction, and everybody wins. Every time, when that happens, I still think, "Ok, what

247

could I have done to make that better, where we don't spend that much time in it."

It's an excellent point as to what I wanted to talk about. I mean, you are running a huge operation, and I know you talk about how much time you spend in your business at "The E-Myth".

Michael, could you expand on how E-Myth keeps running while you are working on other projects?

Sure. We have a Chief Executive Officer at E-Myth, Senior Managers at E-Myth and all of the employees at E-Myth. There are systems constantly being developed to run things smoother. Anybody here could go online to www.E-Myth.com, and they will find a completely exciting world about how to operate a business, how to manage a business, how to grow a business and all the mechanisms in that world that are being invented without me being there.

I spend about three hours a month at E-Myth as Chairman of the Board and Founder...and that's all spent in the board meetings. We discuss strategic issues, issues that are occurring each and every day and growth opportunities – that's the limit of my participation.

That's awesome, Michael.

What I'm doing instead is creating new companies, which will be turn-key companies once they roll out. They're companies that don't require me to be there. All I'm doing is participating in the entrepreneurial role of inventing them.

The first company I'm inventing along

248

those lines is called "The Dreaming Room." As you already know, I have written 7 books, Mark, and they've been extraordinarily successful. But, now I'm off to my next book called, *In The Dreaming Room – Waking The Entrepreneur Within*.

It's a really cool concept...

That's the heart of this new company called "In The Dreaming Room, LLC". Very shortly, someone will be able to go to: www.inthedreamingroom.com and will be able to actually see exactly what the Dreaming Room does and how it works. In the beginning, I'm going to work on the Dreaming Room with would-be entrepreneurs – people who really, really, really want to create a completely new life for themselves. I'm helping them see exactly how to do that.

Up 'til now, I've held eight Dreaming Rooms – the first one in December 2005 and one each month since then. Now, I also have several Dreaming Rooms planned in Canada, a number of them in the United States, several in the U. K.... this thing is going around the world!

It's going to be huge!

Huge! It's bigger than *The E-Myth*. It's absolutely mind-blowing, and the people who have participated in this so far – 25 would-be entrepreneurs – have discovered not only their own business but want to start up a new one. They have participated in these Dreaming Rooms, and it is just blowing their minds as to what is happening to their businesses.

One guy in Canada – a fellow by the name

249

of Peter Leeds – you can see his story on: www.InTheDreamingRoom.com. I'm doing Dreaming Rooms in Vancouver and Calgary, just to name a few. I'll soon be doing Dreaming Rooms in Toronto and Quebec as well.

You'll read stories from people who say, "Wow! I did it, and let me tell you what happened." It's just stunning what's happening to them with all that we do when we go into the Dreaming Room. What I say to people is bring a blank piece of paper and a beginner's mind. Forget about everything you believe to be true. Forget about every problem you think you've got. All I want to do is discuss the biggest, most difficult problem that you've got in the world, and I'm going to show you how to turn that "biggest problem" into your world's most significant, greatest opportunity ...and we're going to do that with each and every person who comes to the Dreaming Room and then let them tell you exactly what happened to them.

Michael, I think I heard this before, or I may have seen it on your website, but you talked about a lady that was working "in" her business, and she was just *done*. She knew she was ready to do something different with her business and with her life. I think I read where she had taken a hiatus for 30 days or so. Is that correct?

Yes. She came into the Dreaming Room, but she couldn't get out of her business....she just couldn't do it. She knew she had to, but she just absolutely couldn't do it. We came to an agreement that she was going to take two weeks off immediately following the Dreaming Room

250

...just two weeks off, but it ended up to be 90 days.

She actually took ninety days off from her business due to what I gave her in that Dreaming Room. I gave her the insight and the commitment and the passion to liberate herself from the business. I told her exactly how to do it, she agreed to do it, and she went away and <u>did</u> it. She even did it with more vigor than I ever imagined.

Then, she came back to another Dreaming Room, and she recorded what happened. She told everybody in that Dreaming Room that her life is completely transformed. Her business is operating better than it ever had before. She happens to be a contractor...a concrete contractor. She's a woman that owns a construction contracting firm and concrete firm, and that's an amazing thing in and of itself. She is on her way to becoming one of the largest companies of her kind in California. She's absolutely determined. She absolutely sees how to do it, and she's even beyond that by now.

Now she "gets" it. Now she doesn't have to kill herself to get to her dream.

You need to understand she was an "E-Myth" fanatic before she came, and now she got something from the Dreaming Room that she didn't get from <u>The E-Myth</u> – she got to have a vision, and she got to have a dream. She now knows that she has to have something that is bigger than life – something pulling and pushing and attracting – she needed to have that, and I understood. I understood because I have felt

251

that passion about *The E-Myth*, and it's the same passion that I brought out to the world.

It's the same passion that I feel when creating and realizing my dream, which is that I want to transform small businesses worldwide. I want to blow people's minds – that's what I do, and that's what we do, as a company. Without a company that has that same passion, there's no way you can do it.

Everything you are saying...it just hits you. I'm sure there are some people reading this and saying to themselves, "This is it!"

Michael, can you give us your website again just so people can have this in front of them? Then, I would like to talk about someone who might be sitting there saying to themselves, "I'm too young" or "I'm too old" or "It's too late" or whatever their thoughts may be. What do you have to say to those people?

"I don't know anything," "I don't know how to do that," "I don't have the money to do that," "I don't have the time to do that," "I don't have your passion to do that"...why not say "I don't know how to do anything"?

"All I know how to do is get up in the morning, brush my teeth, take a shower, have breakfast, go to work"...dreary, dreary, dreary. "I wish I were as smart as you," "I wish I had what you have, but I don't"...and on and on.

What I say to every single one of those people is that all of that is just the excuse you're giving for not letting go and opening yourself up to the possibility that you don't *have* to know anything to begin this process! In fact, when

I started on my vision in 1977 and started my company to do this, I had never owned a company before...I had never done anything like what I am doing now. I didn't know anything about small business when I started.

Honestly, if you asked every small business owner about when they were starting out, I wonder how many of them knew anything about running a business. I bet it's a very small number.

All this started by accident when someone said to me, "Michael, this guy needs your help for creating more sales." It was my friend who'd invited me to meet one of his clients. He had an ad agency, and he didn't know how to convert leads into clients. He said to me, "Michael, why don't you just talk to him", and I said, "But, I don't know anything about his business. In fact, I don't know anything about business at all." He said to me, "Don't worry about it...just trust me. You know more than you think you do."

So, I went to meet this guy, Bob, my friend's client, and we spent an hour together. I started that meeting with that same feeling, "I don't know anything about business. How can I possibly help him if I don't know? He must know a great deal about business because he owns one." Within that hour, Mark, I discovered that both of those assumptions were completely untrue.

I think people underestimate themselves all the time about what they really know.

Well, I did know something about

253

business. Now, let me tell you how strange this is because, of all of the things that I have done previously in my life – I was a saxophone player, a jazz musician, a writer that had never published anything, a carpenter, a house builder, an encyclopedia salesmen, an insurance salesman...I did everything under the sun.

My goodness, you were all over the map!

Oh, yes, I was. I had three masters in my life. One of them was my saxophone teacher, who told me that if I wanted to study with him (I was 9 years old), the first rule of the game was that I had to practice 3 hours a day, 5 days a week, and I had to practice *exactly* what he told me to practice. If I was unwilling to do that, he was uninterested in having me as one of his students. He said, "I only want to teach students who, someday, want to become one of the best saxophone players in the world...that's what I do. And this is what you are going to have to do if you want to study with me." I made the choice and I did it, and, of course, I became an extraordinary saxophone player. That's number one.

My number two master was my sales manager at Encyclopedia Americana. He told me, "You don't need to know anything. In fact, it's best if you don't know anything at all when you start doing this because then I can teach you exactly how to do it. I'm going to give you exactly what you need to be successful at it. I'm going to teach you exactly what you need to say and when you need to say it, and teach you exactly what you need to do. If you do exactly what I say, you'll become as good at doing it as I am. Just

254

practice." That's what he told me.

The guy I studied with on how to build a house told me exactly the same thing. "This is how you do it, and all you have to do is practice exactly what I tell you. Then you go do that, and you will become as good at this as I am."

You don't have to know everything" is what every single one of these guys told me. Well, guess what? Each of those masters in my life taught me that you didn't have to know anything, you just had to *want* to. If you wanted to, they could teach you exactly what to do and exactly what not to do. If you practiced exactly what they told you, everything would happen.

Like my mentor who always says, "You don't have to get it right, you just have to get it going."

So, that's what I said to my first client. I said, "Hell, you don't have a selling system. You need a selling system if you're going to be successful at selling anything so that, when those leads come in, you have a systematic way of responding to them and a systematic way of taking them through the process. There is no process here, but I can do that for you."

So, I went to work on his selling system, which was non-existent, to build one that worked instead of hiring sales engineers. His was a high-tech company, and he said, "I absolutely know that I need sales engineers," to which I said, "You don't need sales engineers, you just need people who will use the system to take your customer to a place where they could finally say 'yes'." And, of course, that is exactly what we did and, guess

255

what, sales went up! He couldn't believe it!

When sales went up, he discovered that he didn't have a financial management system. He wasn't ready for all those sales because he didn't imagine that all of those sales would come in.

He wasn't tapping into the power of his imagination. Anything you can imagine, you can do. Not only that, Michael, but I'm sure you also exposed him to other things that he didn't even realize were missing from his business or that he hadn't even thought of up to that point.

Right – like the fact that he also didn't have a management system or a marketing system or a production system. Then, I began to realize that...wow...*this* is a system. After that, I went to client number one, number two, number three, number four...and I realized they didn't have a vision.

A vision of what, though? A vision of a business that worked. I went to McDonalds, and I saw it, and I said to myself, "My god, I can do that!" Do what? I can build a "McDonalds" with small business consulting. "Why hasn't this ever been done before?" I asked myself, and I answered myself by saying, "What difference does it make, stupid, just do it!" And so I started my company... to create the small business of McDonalds.

And that's exactly what we've done. We've created a turn-key system for consulting with small businesses.

You found a niche. You used what you knew to help others simplify their lives by using systems.

That's exactly what we did, and that's why we have 50,000 plus clients, and that number will keep growing and growing to the many millions of clients that we will have over the next five years. They're actually doing The E-Myth exactly the way I say it. The Dreaming Room, which is what we're talking about now, is the baseline system.

I came to realize that the thing that was missing in The E-Myth – the one thing which is the foundation of The E-Myth – was a way to awaken the entrepreneurial side of every single person out there in the world so that I can show them that there are benchmarks – simple fundamental processes – for creating an extraordinary dream.

At the base of every business is an extraordinary dream. So I am now saying to you, "What's your dream?" Tell me what your dream is. Tell me what's important. Tell me how that's going to transform people worldwide. Tell me why your dream is going to make a difference. We help people begin to explore and expose that and then liven up the passion of that entrepreneur inside of them to get them started in that process.

That, alone, is just so powerful – even just being in the same room with other people facing the same challenges you might be facing. To be around all that energy would be...well, I couldn't even imagine.

I have never even been to a Dreaming Room yet, but I will be at one shortly. I'm sure people have a clearer vision as soon as they walk out of the room, wouldn't you say?

They do. I have had people walk in

depressed, and they walk out mesmerized. It's absolutely stunning. They say, "How in the hell did you do that?" Then you begin to see how you do it...that it's all there waiting to be done. So, I'm saying to people to read this, who are paying this huge "price" of not having their business be what they want or need it to be thatthey don't understand that the genius is already there – the entrepreneur is already there inside of them. All that has to happen is you've got to wake him or her up, and I happen to have a gift for doing that.

That gift is going to be expanded into a turn-key system so that I can replicate this around the world. There will be Dreaming Rooms going on every single day throughout the world, continually awakening the entrepreneurial fire and passion in people to the point that they are either going to be able to finally realize their vision of something extraordinary, of something that needs to be done – some kind of business that they will then be able to invent.

Anybody *can* do it, and everybody *will* be doing it. You can imagine what kind of economic impact that will have on every community, every family, on every state, every country throughout the world. That's what I'm going to do – that's where my passion is.

That is just awesome, Michael. I am really just lost for words right now on your whole process of The Dreaming Room.

While we're talking about it, Michael, do you want to go into explaining more about The Dreaming Room and how it works? Actually, don't you have a website that we talked about earlier

that explains, in detail, what the dreaming room has to offer?

Yes. It's really, really fast and it's really, really simple. You can learn more about The Dreaming Room at our website at www.inthedreamingroom.com/ and also see when and where upcoming events are being held.

What's great about The Dreaming Room is that it's a very small group of intense people who are absolutely committed to transforming their lives. So, I'm saying to you, "Bring a blank piece of paper." As a matter of fact, I'm even going to give them the pad – they don't even have to bring the paper! Bring your beginner's mind. You're going to start your life all over again, and we're going to do it right there in that room. I know that sounds strange, and I know somebody is saying, "Well, how in the world can you do that?" I know that nobody *really* believes their lives are going to be any different or transformed, but...hear me...they *always* are.

Like I said, I will be going to The Dreaming Room myself very soon. Again, Michael, to get more information, where do they need to go?

The website address is: www.inthedreamingroom.com. I want to send you to that website so that you can get a feel for what it is that I'm talking about. You really need to bring someone with you. It doesn't matter who...it can be your wife, your uncle, your aunt, your partner, your cousin, your friend. However, I do have a max of 25 people that can attend any one Dreaming Room, and that's so everyone gets

259

the maximum benefit.

That's amazing. Now, Michael, this can be any type of business owner, right? They don't have to be teachers or lawyers...just any kind of business owner.

It doesn't matter. It can be hi-tech people, low-tech people or no-tech people. We have people who have gotten a job and are thinking about starting a business, and we've got people who have a business and are thinking about getting rid of it for a turn-key.

We have unimaginable people coming in from all over the world. People are coming in from Australia, the UK, and so on and so on, just to be in our Dreaming Rooms.

And this can be a new company, and old company, any kind of company...right, Michael?

It doesn't matter if it's big, small, old or new. All that matters is that you know that there is something missing. There is something missing inside of you. You don't have a dream that keeps you awake at night or you don't have a passion for doing something bigger in life. You don't know *how*, you don't know *why*, and you don't know *what,* but what you <u>do</u> know is that something is missing.

You've got to find something to be passionate about so that you can commit your whole self to transforming your life, your vision and your company so that you can turn it into something significant. It's the significance of it, Mark. That's the deal. That's the passionate purpose of somebody's life. All I'm saying is that we're going to discover it when you come to the Dreaming Room. We do that with every single person that comes to a Dreaming Room.

I know that once they discover their passion, they will know that it isn't peachy every single day. There is a process you'll have to go through, but once you're passionate and committed, there is nothing that can stop you from achieving whatever it is that you're dreaming about.

You're right. The only thing that can stop you is losing your vision and your passion. That is what brings people to the Dreaming Room. Something has happened or they find themselves doing it, doing it, doing it, and it's ordinary, ordinary, ordinary every single day. They're caught up in the disease of work as opposed to the life of creation.

I'm saying that it's the creator within us, the entrepreneur within us, who's wanting to come out, but he or she doesn't know how...they don't know what to do. That's what we do in the Dreaming Room, we dream things in the Dreaming Room to wake people up.

Now, the beautiful part about this, Mark, is that they don't come to buy a dream, you understand? I'm not selling dreams. I'm going to discover – with that person and with all those individuals – what is real for *them*. There is a statement I've heard that says that, "Entrepreneurs don't buy businesses, they create them." You know what I'm saying?

I sure do.

261

What you buy is technology, software or whatever that can run the business that you've created. I'm here to help the entrepreneur within to come out and invent something. I'm not selling business opportunities – there isn't a business opportunity for anybody to be found there.

The opportunity is all around them, everywhere they look. All they have to do is open their eyes, open their minds and open their hearts to begin to understand that the world is full of opportunity, and that's what we're here to create. We want everybody to see the obvious, but, unfortunately, everybody misses the opportunity, and we want him or her to see it...that's what we do.

Absolutely. I know my grandfather always said, "You don't know what you don't know." So, I guess you could say that you don't see what you don't see.

Everyone is just so busy being busy – I guess that's another part of it. Once you start to set these systems up, you have more time to see the opportunities. They literally hit you in the face on a daily basis.

Yes. They're all over the place. Your biggest problem coming out of the Dreaming Room will be that you are flooded with opportunity. It's because your passion gets so aroused. Opportunity is everywhere. They look around and then say, "What do I say 'no' to?" You know what I'm talking about, Mark, because you experience it, and you feel that all the time.

It's an amazing feeling because you can have control of it, and you can turn it on and off whenever you want – it's yours.

I want to touch on something that you said earlier about the McDonalds approach. When you were creating all of this, people called you crazy, right?

Of course...they still do, Mark. They say, "Michael, you're out of your mind. Every business is different, every problem is different, every market is different, every person is different." I'm saying that everything is the same. What an amazing approach when you say that all businesses are the same – meaning that there is a universal way to build a successful company. If that weren't true, then everything would be different. That's not what I set out to do, but we have proved it to be true time and time again.

I know from doing real estate investing that a lot of people say, "You can't do that," or maybe they say, "You're crazy" or whatever they might say...well, don't listen to those people because they're not doing it, so they don't know.

You know what, Mark, you can listen to anybody you want and just smile. Everything they tell you is exactly the opposite of what it usually means anyway. Every single time a naysayer says it can't be done, have them listen to the founder of IBM who said to his son, "I couldn't imagine there being a market for any more than five or six computers worldwide. Somebody at the patent office said that we should close the patent office because everything that was going to be invented already has been." He said that to his son in 1901...it's a true story. Everything has already been invented...imagine...

Do you understand that our world has been completely transformed in the past 50 years? Do you realize that when I was born in 1936 – yes, I'm 70 years old – there wasn't a refrigerator, there wasn't a jet plane, there wasn't television? Do you *get* that? And that list goes on and on and on. Think about it...we don't even know what the world will be like 25 years from now.

Oh, yes, I get it. In just the last five years, we have changed so fast and rapidly. Not only that, but look at the Internet. I refer back to the Internet because the Internet has changed my life for the better and allows me to manage my systems with much more ease.

I do enjoy traveling, and when we started doing that, I really had to figure things out. Going through that process is enlightening because you are going toward your mission, going toward your dream. I wish the Dreaming Room was around back then because I might have been doing this years ago.

This is all just so amazing, and I appreciate you taking the time out of your busy schedule, Michael, to talk with me.

Well, I love it.

Absolutely...me too. All I know is that everyone reading this has got to get into the Dreaming Room. If you can't make it in July, there are many other dates that Michael has available that are coming up.

But, get the book, at least! The book's name is *The E-Myth*. Buy it, and just get it started.

You got it, Mark.

That's the biggest key...80% of your results are from just showing up, but a lot of people just won't show up. And by getting that part right, it will be great. I mean, come on, *Michael* is teaching these — that's a rare situation where you can get *him* teaching you.

You better hurry, guys, because I just turned 70...you never can tell. ..

I would have never guessed that at all. That's an amazing thing...the entrepreneurial life, right?

You got it. You're never too old...you're never too old...

Absolutely! I just want to take a couple more minutes here... You talk about this, and I take it as a key point — everybody talks about wanting to retire. I know my take on this, but can you shine the light on how <u>you</u> feel about the word "retire"?

Mark, that's a dirty word. Why would anybody that is alive and creative and has a spirit inside them want to retire? You want to travel around just to travel around? What's the point? They want to go play golf? What's the point? Some people want to live on the beach...what's the point?

I mean, I am talking about the world is just *waiting* to be transformed. Every human being has the ability to do it – we are born to create. We are born in the image of God. God is the ultimate creator. Man was born to create. We get to create one life – you and I, we get to do that.

I'm 70 years old, and I have 6 new companies. They're sitting there waiting to be done. I'm working on those companies as we speak. There are different options everywhere we look. How could anybody *not* want to become a more significant creator, and then teach their kids how to do that, and then show them that you don't have to take a chump job and be satisfied with it just so you can buy yourself a couple of houses and secure yourself for when you get old and don't want to walk around anymore. I can't even imagine anybody settling for that in their life.

Me neither, which is why I had to touch on that. When somebody says they're retiring, it's like spitting in my face. I can't believe it. It's like the biggest dirty word I hear because, when you're living life on your own terms, why would you ever retire? Like you said, it's silly.

The only reason you would do it is if you felt used up. I am telling you that more people are feeling used up than you can possibly imagine. They are used up because they have done all of the wrong things in their life. They are living a life of scarcity as opposed to abundance, so they feel all used up. They have never experienced the abundance of creation that can come from the inside.

They didn't know that, though, because no one in school ever taught them that. Their parents didn't teach them that, their bosses didn't teach them that, and, most critically, they didn't take that on themselves because they didn't realize they could. They didn't realize they had the capability. They didn't realize they had the genius. They didn't realize they had the imagination. They didn't realize they had a fire in their belly. Fire in your belly comes from tasting the experience of a creation that has come out of you...that is what has given me so much in life.

Michael, I couldn't imagine what my life would be like if I hadn't figured it out...and it all started with *The E-Myth*.

As I work with all of these small companies and see their lives being transformed... they're working significantly *less* and doing significantly *more*. What they need to do is go to www.E-Myth.com and look at all of the stories of the companies that we have transformed. Look at every one of them. There are thousands of stories ...they go on and on and on.

I did all of that, and I started my company at the age of 41 years old. I was 41 when I started down this path. Everybody told me, "You don't have enough money,"...I didn't even have *any* money, and I didn't have any experience. I didn't know anything about what I was about to do, and here I am called "The #1 Small Business Guru Of The Top 5 Most Successful Business Owners In The World" by INC. magazine.

I started at 41, so what's your problem? That's what I'm saying to every single person that's reading now. I'm not here to brag about it...I'm saying that I'm here to share it with you. Well, Mark, I have to go.

Great, thank you for talking with me.

Mark, send your readers to me, and we'll give them some astonishing results.

Thank you, and have a great day.

You have a great day too. I will talk to you soon.

"Ninety-nine percent of failures come from people who have the habit of making excuses."
- George Washington Carver; Botanist

About The Author

Mark Evans DM is the author of many of the top Real Estate Courses available today. He got his start in Real Estate investing by doing landlording and rehabbing, like so many people do, and he's literally done it all, at one point or another. So, after 10 years, he's doing what he started out wanting to do...he's giving back.

But, when he first began his Real Estate Investing career, it started out like probably most people reading this book – he was scattered and unfocused and unsure of how to achieve his dream. He had no zero cash and terrible credit, but was determined to seek out a way to make his dream come true with Real Estate Investing. That's why this book was so important to him to get to you...so that he can help others shave years off of their learning curve and achieve their dreams faster and with less heartache.

Also, like most, he wasn't born with a lot and faced many challenges along the way. He came from a very small town where living paycheck to paycheck was the norm ...and still is. Though, there's nothing wrong with that if that makes you happy, he knew that he wanted a different life for himself. The life he envisioned was one filled with traveling, spending time with his loved ones, taking time out to enjoy his hobbies, writing, reading success books, creating successful students and masterminding with the top coaches of the world, just to name a few.

So, he dove into educating himself about Real Estate investing, made a lot of mistakes along the way, developed many new strategies that helped him to get it right in half the time, and is now living that exact life that he envisioned. You can too, and this book will be a huge stepping stone towards you getting to live _your_ ideal life and realize your dreams, complete with Success, Happiness, Financial Freedom, Abundance, Prosperity and Wealth!

Mark Evans DM wants to congratulate you for taking the step of reading this book and wants to let you know that there IS more to life than living paycheck to paycheck! So, take advantage of the _free_ gifts that we've included at the back of this book and start today.

Mark Evans DM Enjoying the Florida View

"Only those who risk going too far can possibly find out how far one can go."
- T. S. Eliot; Poet

To Receive Your $247 In Free Bonuses: www.TheInsiderSecretsGifts.com

Get Your TWO Free Gifts!

Are You Ready To Become The Next Real Estate Millionaire?

As a thank you for reading this book and helping me to support the charities that are most important to me, I wanted to give you two free gifts, which are valued at more than $247 and are life-changing!

To Get Your Free Gifts Today, Go To:

www.TheInsiderSecretsGifts.com

to claim yours today! My hope is for you to Take Action on everything you have just read and use those tools in harmony with the $247 in free gifts to propel your real estate investing career forward towards huge profits. I'll see YOU on the other side.

FREE BONUS CD

This CD is yours for **FREE**. All I ask is that you pay a non-refundable shipping and handling fee of $2.95 if you are in the U.S. and $4.95 if you are out of the U.S.

Be sure you get the most jaw-dropping CD to come out to the Real Estate Market...ever: **"7 Secrets To Buying And Selling Real Estate From Home With No Cash And No Credit, Even If You're Brand New!"**

◇ Discover how to profit on a property even if it's at a 100% LTV (Loan To Value) and profit greatly from it!

◇ The single most important question you must ask yourself before you get started. (Hint: Not knowing this will almost guarantee your failure!)

Make a copy of this page, fill it out and fax it in to 614-474-1492.

Name _____

Address _____

City _____ State _____ Zip _____

Phone _____ Fax _____

Credit Card   □ Visa   □ MasterCard   □ Discover   □ AmEx

Credit Card # _____ Exp Date _____

Security Code _____ Email _____

Signature _____ Date _____

To Receive Your $247 In Free Bonuses: www.TheInsiderSecretsGifts.com

Contacting The Author

Mark Evans DM has a busy schedule - working his Real Estate Investing business and traveling across the world with his family...all while continuing to strive for excellence in business as well as in helping his students propel forward to become more profitable, all through using systems.

However, he is always looking for opportunities to help those individuals that understand that success is a lifestyle. Those who are committed to achieving their goals may have the chance to take advantage of Mark's coaching, books, teleseminars and live workshops. Please contact Mark's office at the web address below to see if you qualify for his available programs.

Mark Evans DM may also be available for speaking and seminar engagements, mentoring, consulting, marketing and/or interviews, both for TV and radio.

To contact Mark Evans DM directly,
go to www.MarkEvansDM.com

Websites You Need To Know About

- For your bonuses, go to www.TheInsiderSecretsGifts.com

  - Bonus: I have included an un-advertised bonus, but you must to go www.TheInsiderSecretsGifts.com to get it

- Discover Why Everything You've Learned About Real Estate Investing Is Backwards

  - www.ReverseRealEstate.com

- Work less. Make more. Let the internet make your life easier and more profitable. Are you using the internet to do your real estate deals? Go to:

  - www.DiscountRealEstateWebsites.com

- Have profitable deals sent to you via your email inbox

  - www.WholesaleRealEstateDeals.com

- Get the most complete course offered today on "Subject To" investing. Go to:

  - www.Sub2Magic.com

- Get the same business card that I use daily, and it helps me do an extra 3-4 deals every year just for having it. Go to:

  - www.DiscountREInvestorBizCards.com

- Discover the techniques I still use today that helped me to be financially free before the age of 30 — go to:

  - www.GotThePowerOfConcentration.com

- We'll help you keep your finger on the pulse of the Real Estate market. For up to the minute market information go to:

  - www.MarkEvansDM.com

- Are you among the 500 Real Estate Investors who are committed to success?

  - www.500RealEstateInvestorNames.com

Mark Evans DM Enjoying the Florida View

Here are some checks from some of my current students who are using my systems...

To Receive Your $247 In Free Bonuses: www.TheInsiderSecretsGifts.com